12.00

ANYONE
CAN HAVE A
HAPPY CHILD

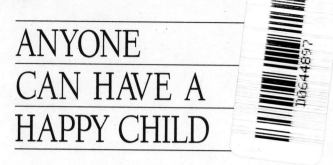

NO LONGER PROPERTY OF
RESCIA COLLEGE LIBRARY

ANYONE
CAN HAVE A

*How to Nurture
Emotional Intelligence*

HAPPY CHILD

Jacob Azerrad, Ph.D.

M. EVANS AND COMPANY, INC. • *New York*

BRESCIA COLLEGE LIBRARY
OWENSBORO, KENTUCKY

Copyright © 1980, 1997 by Jacob Azerrad, Ph.D.

All rights reserved. No part of this book may be reproduced or transmitted in any form or by any means without the written permission of the publisher.

M. Evans and Company, Inc.
216 East 49th Street
New York, New York 10017

Library of Congress Cataloging-in-Publication Data

Azerrad, Jacob, 1936–
    Anyone can have a happy child : how to nurture
emotional intelligence / Jacob Azerrad. — 2nd ed.
      p. cm.
    ISBN 0-87131-810-5
    1. Parenting   2. Child psychology   3. Child rearing
I. Title
 HQ755.8.A97   1997
649' .1—dc21   97-4935
                                               CIP

649.1
A993

Designed and composed by *John Reinhardt Book Design*

Manufactured in the United States of America

9 8 7 6 5 4 3 2 1

To Sandy, with Love.
You taught me, through family; friends; and,
above all, your caring, that "Love and Work"
is what life is all about.

93226

CONTENTS

PREFACE

The original title of this book was *Raising Children Positively*. At the suggestion of my publisher it was changed to *Anyone Can Have a Happy Child*. I admit that I had doubts about the title at that time. I no longer have doubts; in fact, this is exactly what this book is all about. It is what all parents want for their children and it is what many parents have said to me in just those words. Thomas Jefferson said that we have the "unalienable Right" to "the Pursuit of Happiness." This book will give parents the tools to pursue and achieve this goal for their child.

But happiness is a vague term. Just what is happiness? What is a happy child? For many decades those in my profession have taken us down the "understanding" path, which all too often has led to "understanding" and precious little behavior and feeling change. They have, in the process, been responsible for a theory of behavior which overlooks a very important key to happiness. They have encouraged us to look for deep-rooted unconscious meanings underlying behavior, and have meanwhile overlooked the behaviors themselves. Behaviors are the key to happiness, because they are the building blocks of feelings of self worth, feelings which, in the final analysis, will make it unnecessary to spend years looking for that so-called inner child.

Many years ago a man named Sigmund Freud said that the two most important things in life were "lieben und arbeiten," love and work. He was on target, but his methods provide little in the way of how to achieve success in these two crucial areas of living. Behaviors are the key to achieving success in both love and work, behaviors which will put your child in touch with the many joys of living in these two essential areas of human life; human relationships (love) and achievement (work).

I look upon behavior, in its simplest terms, as the individual's attempt to make life more satisfying, to put zip and enjoyment into life in the best way he or she knows. Sometimes, the "best" way the individual knows is an inappropriate way, and the result, very often, is an unhappy person. Other times, an individual's behavior is the kind that draws warmth, caring, and success—things that can mean happiness.

During my thirty years as a clinical psychologist working with the families of children who have learned inappropriate behaviors, I have gradually developed the methods described in this book. They help parents become *better* parents by showing them how to teach their children ways to behave that will put them in touch with the multitude of satisfactions our world has to offer. The methods are both effective and easily learned, so much so that it is not uncommon for parents to come to me after only a few sessions and tell me that the problem we had discussed a few weeks earlier is no longer a problem. Almost invariably they add, ". . . and we haven't done anything differently."

In reality, they have done something differently. It has had a major impact on their child's behavior and feelings, yet it is so simple and so grounded in common sense that it is difficult for parents to believe that they have actually been instrumental in causing a real and lasting change. These methods, too, are not only effective in working with the child with behavior problems; they also provide all parents with ways to teach values and the many positive behaviors they want their children to acquire in the process of growing up.

The thinking that forms the basis for the methods described in this book is the result of two convergent influences. My initial training in psychoanalytic theory taught me to look at behavior within the context of the total person, rather than as an isolated component of that person. However, this way of thinking, while providing the attitude with which I deal with children's problems, does not provide effective answers to the questions of changing behaviors and feelings. The methods I use then derive from the second influence, my behavioral training.

The child who is disruptive and who turns off other children (and parents as well) by his behaviors should not be looked upon as an angry child, but rather as one who is reaching out for human contact. He has learned ways that bring people closer, but in *anger* rather than because they feel warmth and caring towards him. He must first learn behavior that will bring people closer because they care about him, behavior that will bring warmth and *affection*. Then we can help him learn to give up those behaviors that bring him the immediate but lesser satisfaction of *attention*. Other children, possibly because of painful past experiences with people, turn inward for their satisfactions. They become withdrawn and isolated; they set up an internal "Disneyland" and escape into a world of fantasy that cuts them off from life's real rewards. They, too, can be taught behaviors that draw warmth and caring from the world around them.

Most important for all children, an appropriate repertoire of behaviors helps to build a strong internal foundation for happiness that lasts far beyond childhood through an entire lifetime. This is a sense of self-esteem, feelings of self-worth that parents can nurture and that are the ticket of admission into the world of satisfaction, success, and happiness.

—JACOB AZERRAD, PH.D.
Lexington, Massachusetts
1997

ACKNOWLEDGMENTS

There are a great many individuals without whom this book would never have become a reality. Among them, Dr. Joel Greenspoon, whose understanding of human behavior took me from the demon haunted world of psychoanalytic mythology to a man of science by the name of Fred Skinner; Dr. Wallace A. Kennedy, whose encouragement throughout my graduate training was an invaluable source of strength; Richard Barrows, who has always been a source of encouragement and sincere words of appreciation; Anne Borchardt, my literary agent, who initially recognized the worth of the original manuscript; George de Kay, my publisher, whose belief in my book made its revised edition a reality; and Susan Buckley, for her many tireless hours of work on revisions and corrections, and for her attention to detail and sense of humor.

Last, but surely not least, there are two other individuals without whom this book could never have become a reality. Henry Scammell, who took the original book, revisions, and corrections, and, with good humor and excellent skill, transformed it into its present, very readable and enjoyable form. The late Professor B. F. Skinner had a major impact on my thinking as well as my ability to write this book. It was his invitation to attend his talk on writing behavior at the Learning Center, Harvard University, that enabled me to complete the manuscript in original form in five months.

Chapter One

ANYONE CAN HAVE
A HAPPY CHILD

It's true: anyone *can* have a happy child. But that doesn't mean everyone will get one. Nowhere does it say that happiness is something we or our children automatically deserve in life just for showing up.

It's not guaranteed by the Constitution or protected by law. It's not an entitlement like social security.

And if you're a careful reader of the Declaration of Independence, you know that happiness is *not* one of our inalienable rights, along with life and liberty, cited by Thomas Jefferson.

What Jefferson did include as a right was "the *pursuit* of happiness." He knew it was something that must be worked at to be achieved, and whether for our children or ourselves, it comes only with effort.

A lot of people don't understand that. Psychologists tell them to follow their instincts in raising their children, but this is nonsense; there are no instincts for dealing with most of the requirements of child rearing. The process involves learned behavior. It involves parent selection. Instincts or natural selection will in no way make for a happy child.

"Happiness" and "unhappiness" aren't easy to define, because they're words with many meanings. They're interpretive rather than objective words. We use them to express our interpretations of the results of behavior, rather than its causes, and in this lies the key to raising a happy child.

Happiness comes from the most precious gift a parent can give a child—the gift of appropriate behavior. As we help our children to take over responsibility for their lives and teach them how to become happy, successful adults, we succeed for ourselves as well. That's how happiness works.

This book is about the pursuit of happiness. It will help you to equip your child with the skills, habits, and security all children need to seek and find fulfillment.

And by helping you to be a more effective parent, it should help you find more happiness for yourself.

THERE ARE CERTAIN RULES . . .

Whether you believe in God, the Darwinian theory of evolution, or both, it's obvious that the human race has been equipped with a number of mechanisms for the survival of the species. One is our appetite for food. Another is our sex drive. A third is the nurture of our offspring.

By themselves, our instincts have no relationship to having a happy child—or, for that matter, to being a happy adult.

To a degree, our appetite for food, our sex drive, and the impulse to nurture our children are instinctive—but there are limits. Instinct doesn't tell us how to handle a knife and fork, it doesn't instruct us in the protocols of dating, and it doesn't always tell us how to give our children the kinds of love and discipline they need to fulfill themselves and prosper. For those things, humans have been blessed with the ability to learn.

In support of that ability, Whoever made us has given us a very powerful brain, far and away superior to that of any other species. Thanks to this attribute, we've been able to go to the moon and back safely, to build bridges over large rivers and buildings that reach the sky, and to instantaneously send color pictures halfway around the world.

In addition, we live in an orderly, lawful universe—day follows night, winter follows summer, Halley's comet comes every seventy-six years, the tides roll in and out twice daily. Man used his brain to predict many of these patterns in nature thousands of years before the first computer.

So, with all these things going for us, how come we have such a hard time getting along with one another and bringing up our children?

The answer is that most of us haven't applied all that brainpower to understanding the messages in our genes and learning the simplest lessons about the role of natural consequence in human relationships. There's a lot of needless pain and suffering in this world simply because we still haven't learned to deal effectively with how we behave.

We are all equally subject to the same simple, natural laws. But many of us still are unaware of the powers they have in our lives, and fewer yet know how to make them work to our advantage.

We haven't learned to create happiness.

OUT-THINKING COMMON SENSE

A major reason we don't understand our behavior is because there have been many complicated, laughable, and sometimes frightening fictions about why people act the way they do.

The ancient Greeks thought our fates were ordained in a kind of lottery by the balance among our various natural humors.

The Puritans in seventeenth-century Salem explained alarming, evil, or eccentric behavior in terms of witches, demons, and possession.

Sigmund Freud told us our behavior is the result of unconscious forces with names like id, ego, and superego, all fighting like old-world gods in our heads and for our souls.

Much of what we think we know about ourselves was written by false prophets. Most human behavior has precious little to do with "humors"; ids, egos, and superegos; or demons and possession.

Instead, it has everything to do with something so disarmingly simple that almost no one paid much attention to it until just recently. It has to do with learning.

LEARNING AND THE LAW OF CONSEQUENCE

Three centuries ago, Isaac Newton observed that for every action there is an equal and opposite reaction. His Third Law of Motion could apply equally well to the dynamics of human behavior. We learn by recognizing the consequences, both good and bad, that follow from the ways we act.

With sex, the positive consequences of emotionally intelligent actions range from physical gratification and a loving relationship to the preservation of our species. Positive consequences from an intelligent diet can be good health and a long life. Emotionally intelligent parenting liberates our children's potential and enriches all our lives.

Mature, successful people determine what they do and how they do it based on their understanding of natural consequence. If we put our food in the fire, it tastes better and is more more healthful to eat, but if we put our hand in the fire we get burned. We can wear clothes of fabric made from the cotton plant but not from poison ivy. There are limits to how high we can climb without risk or how far we can fall without injury.

For children, the most potent natural consequences, the ones that teach them the most about their early life and that set the pattern for what comes later, are the consequences related to senses and feelings.

All parents want happiness for their children. The one way to ensure they get it is for the parents to provide the child with a world that nurtures the behavior that produces happiness.

Self-esteem, for example, is one result of parents giving a child an appropriate repertoire of behaviors. What children think of themselves owes first and foremost to the ways in which they are treated by their parents, especially in the nurture of appropriate behaviors. Any parent can produce fantastic improvements in the ways a child behaves, sometimes nearly overnight, just by creatively changing the ways in which they respond to their children's behavior.

LOVE AND WORK

Sigmund Freud is not one of the people I worship, but when he says that the two essentials for maturity are love and work, I agree with him. Love in the broadest sense of the term is people skills—how to get along with others, how to relate to those around us in a way that leads to success and happiness.

These skills are a big part of what Daniel Goleman refers to as Emotional Intelligence. Children who learn emotionally intelligent behavior will succeed better in this world than those whose intelligence is measured simply by IQ.

The other essential is work.

A child's first job is to learn the world. With the right encouragement, the joy of endless discovery will lead to a lifelong thirst for learning. It will also lead to a sense of purpose and even more importantly of self-worth. Successful children develop an early sense that their lives are meaningful to others, that they can make a difference, that their destiny on this planet is to serve a useful goal—a sense that doesn't need to have any connection at all to a young child's decision to be a cowboy one day or a nurse the next.

Love and work don't exist in a vacuum; they function through behavior, which is something children learn from their parents. Parents, in turn, have to learn simple, natural techniques for nurturing a behavioral repertoire in their children that will lead to success in love and work. What I teach parents is how to nurture behaviors that will lead to success in these two basic areas of life.

You, too, can learn the behaviors that will reward your child's life, now and through adulthood, with success and satisfaction.

"NOTICE ME"

In the infant, there are two types of crying—respondent and operant—and they serve two purposes. Respondent crying is a result of prior events. It's what happens when an infant is hungry, in pain, in need of a diaper change, or is experiencing some other unpleasant thing that causes him to protest in the only available way. The respondent cry says, "Help end the pain or discomfort I am experiencing. Take care of me."

The other kind of crying says, "Notice me—I need your love, your kisses, I want to have human contact." Operant is the word for behavior that's controlled by consequences. Most behavior is operant.

If we were talking right now, your subtle show of interest or impatience would control my behavior. If you nod and smile in encouragement or agreement, my own enthusiasm will increase, perhaps along with the speed of my speech and the level of my voice. If you keep looking about the room or at your watch, or if you start yawning, the tone and volume will decrease or stop. Partners in conversation generally regulate each other's behavior by consequences.

Salesmen override the operant signals they get in conversation until they bring you around to the consequence they want. It doesn't come naturally, and they have to train themselves to stay focused on their own agenda. In a presidential debate, for example, Kennedy and Nixon or Clinton and Dole rehearse for hours to avoid responding to powerful operant challenges from their adversaries. In normal conversation, those signals would divert them to questions other than the ones each of them wanted to answer.

If we relate to our children in the incomplete or one-way mode of a sales pitch or a debate, the results can be costly.

Many years ago, a study of two groups of women who gave birth in prison dramatically illustrated what can go wrong when children's lives are governed by unnatural rules and they receive inappropriate responses to fundamental needs.

In one prison, it happened that living arrangements allowed the children to be in the same rooms with their mothers. In the other, authorities decided things would work better if the children were separated from their mothers at birth and cared for by nurses. All the children in both groups were given everything they wanted or needed in the way of food, clothing, heat, and shelter, but while the mother-child relationship in the first prison was one-to-one, in the other the ratio of nurses to their tiny charges was about one-to-twelve.

Because of that disparity, and because the maternal bond supplies a far stronger impulse than even the best of intentions, the allocation of hugs and physical affection differed widely as well. The children in the first prison were picked up and fussed over all the time; those in the second hardly at all.

All of the children who were cared for by their mothers completed the study. Of those who received their care from nurses, more than one child out of every three was dead before the study ended. There was no meanness involved, and no overt abuse. What had happened was that "notice me" behavior was largely ignored, partly because of logistical differences and partly because a parent has far more of a naturally physical relationship with a child than a paid provider does. The cause of death was nothing more sinister than the most common form of neglect.

Operant crying is just one form of behavior that says the infant is in need of those essentials. If the need is continuously unmet, the tears will eventually stop as the child grows older, only to be replaced by other behavior that also says, "Notice me."

There are two reasons parents should give their child attention: for nothing, just because they love the child, and to nurture behavior that will make the child proud.

THE GIFT OF BEHAVIOR

We give our child the gift of behavior when we nurture those first words, "Mama, Dada." We give it when we call Grandma in the presence of our child to share developmental landmarks such as first steps or special events, or just to give words to our love. The ability to communicate is an essential tool by which children find happiness, and we encourage this form of behavior by demonstrating how it is done and with notice and praise for their progress in developing skills of their own.

Very few parents need to be told to nurture speaking. It comes naturally. Nor do we need to tell parents to nurture those first steps or the first smiles. The result of that nurture is a child who never stops talking or walking, and hopefully, who never stops smiling.

However, smiling requires more than the nurturing of smiling behavior—we need to encourage those actions that lead to smiles of pride and success. We need to nurture those behaviors that will create happiness.

It isn't always easy. We live in a beautiful but complex world, a world that has the potential to give us much happiness but also much pain and suffering. So how can we as parents maximize our children's happiness and minimize the hurt?

We start by identifying what our child needs to learn as part of the growing-up process. We need to teach our children those behaviors that will bring satisfaction in our world. We need to teach them to love and to work.

Consider the period we arbitrarily call the Terrible Two's. This is nothing more than the time when a child still hasn't learned that we live in a world where we can't always have what we want. To deal with the Terrible Two's—with the child's difficulty in learning to handle frustration—I teach parents to nurture behavior that demonstrates taking disappointment calmly.

That nurture has to take the form of more than praise. Praise is over in a few seconds. Parents need to keep a diary of their child's positive behaviors, and then later, maybe after an hour, take the time to explicitly nurture them. "You were at Johnny's house playing, and I know you wished you could play there all day long. But when it was time to leave, you said goodbye, got your coat, and went home calmly. That was very grown-up, and I'm proud of you. You handled that disappointment like a real big boy."

Children most often assimilate this information silently, but they remember that they get exactly the kind of attention they need—approval, love—after they have engaged in those behaviors they need to learn. The attention isn't something transient that ends with the event, but a time-delayed response that extends the gratification and anchors the memory of that behavior in the other parts of their lives. They're getting noticed in a positive way for taking disappointment calmly, and for them the best part is that it affirms they are growing up.

CHILDREN WITHOUT FRIENDS

When children are cut off from those around them, they tend to become self-involved and to see the almighty Me as the center of the world. Children who have no friends must be taught through nurture how to take themselves out of the center and focus instead on others—I refer to this other-centeredness as Mother Theresa behavior. In cases of sibling rivalry, it means the nurturing of sibling caring.

Although the nineteenth-century axiom that "children should be seen but not heard" may sound today like a recipe for disaster, don't write off its very valid point. The behaviors that parents need to give their children are quiet ones that don't demand notice or call attention to themselves. Parents have to be sensitized to these very precious quiet behaviors and how to nurture them. Otherwise, children realize that if they can't get attention for appropriate behaviors, they can always get it by rocking the boat. The most important two things I do for parents are to help them identify the problem areas, and then teach them to nurture appropriate behavior at the same time they avoid nurturing behaviors that are meant to disrupt or shock.

WE'RE NOT AS SPECIAL
AS WE'D LIKE TO THINK

Sometimes when I consider all the mythology my profession has developed to explain why people behave the ways they do, I'm ashamed to call myself a psychologist. Why not take nature at face value? We can laugh now and feel superior to our ancestors for how they reacted when it was suggested that the earth was not the center of the solar system, but we still see the same thinking around us every day. Why else did President Clinton's advisors tell him to invoke the national security about possible evidence of life on Mars?

I suspect the biggest reason that many people are reluctant to accept Darwinian theory is because we still can't let go of the view of humankind as special on this earth and in this universe. That was certainly why Galileo was prosecuted by the Inquisition, and it has a lot to do with why the Pope didn't get around to forgiving him for some four hundred years after he was vindicated by science. Darwin was smart enough to describe mankind as "the wonder and glory of the universe," but it didn't win him a lot of friends when he used the same occasion to suggest we stand just one rung up the ladder from the monkeys.

"Some people are uncomfortable with the idea that humans belong to the same family of animals as cats, cows and raccoons," Phil Donahue says in his book, *The Human Animal*. "It doesn't sound dignified enough. They're like the people who become successful and then don't want to be reminded of the old neighborhood."

When B. F. Skinner told us our behavior isn't special—it's driven by the same laws of learning as the lower animals—it didn't win him any popularity contests. But the fact remains, we're a part of this universe and in some ways not as special as we'd like to think.

It may be that one of the reasons there's so much pain in the world is because as animals we have a built-in flaw: to survive in the wild we had to be supremely sensitive to danger, to things that were shocking and potentially injurious or deadly—and humans who lacked that sensitivity in their genetic code did not survive. As a result, we're not nearly as sensitive to things that are quiet.

When we nurture quiet behaviors, Skinner says, we need to remember that the process is a silent one, and be deliberate in our positive reinforcement. In nurturing noisy behaviors, by contrast, we don't need to use our brain, because it's in our genetic code.

REWRITING YOUR CHILD'S FUTURE EMOTIONAL HISTORY

Our animal legacy notwithstanding, each of us is born with our own individual temperaments and characters, upon which our experience is imposed, and as a species we are highly dependent on learning.

Parents have a unique relationship with their children, which shapes and sets their ways of thinking for a lifetime. What parents say and do can make the child and future adult proud and self-confident and happy—or just the opposite. The positive feelings a parent plants in a child's heart all last just as long as the negative input that can warp and destroy.

I work with adults all the time who have serious problems because they are carrying painful, heavy baggage from childhood. They still believe, despite major contradictory evidence, that they're stupid, ugly, unlovable, unworthy—because their own parents told them that when they were children, at a time when cognitions were immature and emotions were dominant. Even using behavioral techniques, I have difficulty changing old tapes from the past.

There's a period when every child's intellectual cognition is very primitive and they learn through their emotions, on the level of feelings. At that period in life, when parents criticize them and make negative comments, they imprint belief systems that last a lifetime and are terribly resistant to change. Years after, even though the children are now grown and may even know intellectually that some of those things they learned are false, lies stamped in indelible ink on the maps given them as children still determine the ways they feel about themselves and how they behave.

If parents can learn to encourage their children's positive behaviors—to cultivate the nurture response—before their children are teenagers, they can use it to print a map with truth and love that will lead their children along the safe, happy pathways where they were meant to live their lives.

Chapter Two

CHILDREN DON'T NEED PSYCHOLOGISTS; THEY NEED PARENTS

You are your children's best teacher and their best therapist.

Bobby, for example, may be terrific at making and keeping friends, or he may alienate every kid he meets. If he's good at socializing, it's a certainty he learned a lot of what he knows from his parents. And if he's not, he may not even know he has a problem that needs to be solved. The chances are a lot better that it will be his parents, not Bobby, who spot the trouble and try to do something about it.

All parents want what is best for their children.

They want them to have friends; to do well in school; to learn responsibility; to be honest, loving, and kind; and to think well of themselves. They want their children to be happy.

Parents want these things for their children, no matter what they themselves are like, or what they think their own failings are.

There are no "bad" parents. None of them sets out deliberately to harm their child, even if they have problems of their own in dealing with life. Even if they don't think of themselves as happy adults, they always hope to have happy children, with strong values and open to all the satisfactions life has to offer.

How about being "better" parents, then? The main reason

parents seek professional advice is because they need someone to explain clearly and simply why their children behave as they do. They need to understand the role parents actually play in bringing them up, giving direction to their behavior, and teaching them what kind of behavior is appropriate and valued.

Children's behavior, good or bad, is directly related to the consequences of that behavior. In almost every instance, it is worthwhile for them to behave as they do. As a consequence of their behavior they are rewarded with time and attention and a heavy degree of parental involvement. It doesn't matter to children whether they're being rewarded for behavior adults think is bad or good. In either case, the rewarded behavior is likely to continue. It's up to parents to be selective about the behavior that receives this kind of positive attention, because prior to the teenage years, a child's parents are the most influential people in his or her life.

By understanding the reality of your child's behavior, by differentiating your response appropriately, and by using your great powers of praise and approval, you can be a better parent—and you can have a happy child.

WHERE'S BILLY?

This is the key to all the recommendations I make to parents who consult me about behavioral difficulties. Although I am a "child psychologist," I seldom meet face to face with the children with whom I am working. I usually never see the child at all, although sometimes a mother will bring out a snapshot and say, "You must see what Billy looks like." By the end of our relationship, even though Billy has never set foot in my office, his mother assures me that his behavior has shown a marked improvement. Instead of having spent endless hours playing games with Billy and talking with him about his behavior, I have taught his mother and father to be his teachers and/or "therapists."

It is a method that works. The principles I teach parents can be applied by anyone to raising children, and they can help parents help children who have learned negative behaviors (and who are most likely to be "unhappy" children) discover new and more satisfying ways of behaving.

You are your child's best teacher. Bobby's not going to love a therapist or psychologist; if he doesn't have a natural bond with his care provider, he doesn't *need* or want that person's attention and approval. He wants love and attention from his parents. He usually isn't interested even in talking about his behavior with a therapist. Very likely he's already getting that from Mom and Dad. Finally, he isn't interested in wasting play time to visit the office of a man or woman he scarcely knows. He'd rather be spending it doing something he enjoys.

The office setting is an artificial one for a child. The place where he or she shows behavior problems is at home, or school; the consequences of behavior occur at home, too, where the time, attention, and praise for positive behavior, or correction of negative behavior, should come from the people who count most—the parents.

Parents are often surprised that I am able to work with children I seldom meet.

"Don't you really need to see the child?" they ask. "How can you rely on what a mother or father tells you?"

I can rely very much on parental observations if the parents learn to look at the reality of the behavior rather than to interpret what a behavior means.

For example, a mother may say that her child is jealous, immature, irresponsible, shy, sad, hyperactive, angry, depressed. The child "hates school" or "doesn't trust me." Any one of these words describing behavior may mean different things to different people.

Exactly what does "jealous" mean to a particular mother of a particular child? It means not just that the child seems to have feelings that are jealous, but that she does specific things: "She throws her toys or has a tantrum when I pay attention to the baby." That objective description of a kind of behavior that expresses jealousy identifies the ways in which the mother wants her child to change: no more tantrums, no more thrown toys.

What does a mother mean by "immature"? She defines it by saying she wants Billy to be more "grown-up." How do these two abstract words translate into concrete actions? She has to look at Billy's specific behavior to determine what she means by "immature" and pinpoint actions that are "grown-up."

Billy's eight and he won't tie his shoes, although he knows how; Mother has to do it for him. He needs help getting dressed. He won't pick up after himself when he's asked to. Now it's easy for Mother to see specific manifestations of immaturity she wants to change: she wants him to do things for himself, keep his room neat—in short, do the things that mean "grown-upness."

SEEING YOUR CHILD WITH NEW EYES

Being objective about problem behaviors is the first part of learning to look at your child with the kind of perspective that permits change. There's a second, even more important part. You must also learn to look at your child with eyes that see the quiet, valuable, and beautiful behaviors that are always there in miniature. All too often, those behaviors go unnoticed and unencouraged because we pay more attention to behavior that makes waves.

Sometimes a child's efforts to be grown-up and responsible, to show caring, to make friends, to learn new things, are so ordinary to adult eyes and so fleeting that they pass us by or are forgotten the next moment. If the behavior is unnoticed or forgotten, the child has no way of knowing that this is behavior the parents consider valuable and appropriate. He or she may repeat the behavior by chance, but isn't likely to repeat it just because you want him to, if the behavior hasn't been encouraged within the home.

If good news all too often means no news, bad news (or bad behavior) gives us something to talk about, and we do. "Bad" behavior seldom passes by without comment.

If Polly sits down to dinner and eats what's in front of her, nobody at the dinner table is going to notice. If Polly dumps her plate on the floor and refuses to eat, she's going to get an immediate response. People are going to pay attention. Yet the attention itself encourages Polly to do the same thing at the next meal. Logically, if she were to receive similar notice for cleaning her plate without a fuss, she'd do it regularly.

In the first case, in spite of the attention, she can't be called happy. In the second, with her parents responding positively to this ordinary, expected, and positive behavior, she is more likely to be.

"WHAT ARE WE DOING WRONG?"

When Johnny's mother looks out the kitchen window on a spring afternoon, she notices that Johnny and Freddy, the boy from next door, are tossing a Frisbee around. Then she sees what she sees too frequently these days: Johnny is insisting that he take a second throw because he doesn't like the outcome of his first throw. Freddy protests. They're supposed to be taking turns. Now Johnny becomes angry because he's not going to get his way. He calls Freddy a name and hits him. That's the last straw for Freddy, who picks up his Frisbee and goes home. It happens all the time.

"What am I going to do with the boy?" Johnny's mother says in despair. "He's only nine, but he sure knows how to lose friends, if he manages to make them at all."

When Johnny trails into the house, she sits him down at the kitchen table.

"Johnny, for about the hundredth time, how do you think you're going to have any friends if you don't play fair?"

Johnny shrugs.

93226   649.1   Brescia College Library
A993   Owensboro, Kentucky

"Someday Freddy won't come back at all if you're not nicer. How would you like it if Freddy treated you that way? Doesn't it make you unhappy not to have any friends?"

Johnny admits that he's unhappy. He doesn't know why he behaves that way.

"I wish you'd tell me what's bothering you," his mother says. "Something must be, that you can't get along with other kids. Are you worried about something?"

Johnny's willing to talk about it, but they don't seem to be getting anywhere toward solving his problem. Fifteen or twenty minutes later, Johnny's mother is talked out. Maybe it's done some good. She hopes so, because a nine-year-old who can't get along with other boys his age has a problem.

A couple of days later, Freddy is persuaded to come back to Johnny's house with a couple of other boys for a game of baseball. Mother's watching the game from the window again, and when Freddy pitches a perfect strike to catcher Johnny, Johnny can be heard shouting, "Great pitch!" The game proceeds peacefully, and for once there's no trouble.

This day, when Johnny comes in, his mother is busy with something. She doesn't mention the game; after all, it went just the way a baseball game should.

"Who won?" she asks.

"Freddy and I did," Johnny says, and he's sent off to amuse himself until dinnertime. He finds his sister quietly coloring byherself and ends up pestering her until their mother puts a stop to it.

"Johnny," she says, "what gets into you? You know you're bothering Lisa. Can't you even get along with your own sister? I want you to go to your room and stay there until I call you for dinner. I've had just about enough from you."

Johnny's mother is a kind and caring woman, she doesn't alienate her friends, little Lisa gets along well with children, Johnny's father has no trouble getting along with people, yet Johnny has difficulty making and keeping friends. How has he learned this kind of behavior?

"What are we doing wrong?" his parents ask. "Are we bad parents who don't know how to raise our son? Haven't we set a good example?"

Johnny's parents are asking the wrong questions, of themselves and of their son. The questions parents should ask are: What do I see when I look at my child? What do I comment on? What kind of behavior do I nurture? Johnny in an argument with Freddy? Or Johnny calling out, "Great pitch!"? Polly refusing to eat her dinner once again and throwing a tantrum when told she has to? Or Polly eating quietly, perhaps agreeing to try a new kind of food, even though she's not sure she's going to like it? A child who mopes around and claims to be depressed? Or a mostly cheerful child who is happy?

Do you see—in a way that really registers in your mind—what is called "bad" behavior, the kind that causes the most turmoil in the family and always gets a response from you? Do you fail to see the good and positive behavior that every child displays at least occasionally, because it is so expected, so ordinary, and so brief that it passes you by and is soon forgotten?

If so, then that's what you're doing wrong.

It's easy to fix.

HOW TO GET WHAT YOU ASK FOR

Let's go back for a moment to Freddy and Johnny and his mother.

Johnny's problem behavior with his friend did get a lot of attention. Not only did Freddy go home, but Johnny's mother wasted a good deal of her time talking to her son about it. Those fifteen or twenty minutes they spent discussing what was causing Johnny to behave that way were fifteen or twenty minutes of Mother's undivided attention.

The peaceful baseball game, on the other hand, passed without comment. Johnny's mother didn't do more than acknowledge that it happened. For all practical purposes, she didn't "see" what was going on, although she was watching.

The message to Johnny is clear: negative behavior means attention—all that time and talk, a response. There's no reward for behaving well, for doing the things that result in making friends with Freddy and the other boys. He might as well annoy his sister; that's a sure attention-getter.

This simple little scenario isn't rare. You notice disruptive behavior, and you want to stop it, either as it's happening or by getting to the cause so that it won't happen again. Parents resort to a variety of methods to do this. The immediate response is yelling, anger, reprimands, and some form of punishment if the situation is serious enough. Often it means a discussion of the behavior with the child, in an effort to get to the problems behind it. Then the parents wonder why nothing seems to work, especially when the child turns around the next day and does the very same thing. The result is unhappy children and unhappy parents.

All of these methods for dealing with behavior problems mean that time and attention are being devoted exclusively to the child. And children love attention, never more so than when it comes from those most important people in their lives, their parents. They don't necessarily worry about the nature of the behavior that gets the attention.

What I try to teach parents is that it is just as easy to nurture positive behavior as it is the opposite kind, and they can get the behavior they ask for when they know how to ask. Attention and encouragement can just as easily be given to "good" (valued) behavior—grown-upness, being a good friend, being responsible, generous, honest, and thoughtful—if you learn to see it when it occurs, and if you know how to use the power of praise you have as a parent. If you make valued behaviors worthwhile to the child, the child is going to repeat them. As you praise him, you enhance his feelings of self-esteem, and the child begins to feel he is a worthwhile person.

A child who has feelings of self-worth, who cares about himself, is a happy child.

Chapter Three

THE WITCHES OF ID

There is a longstanding, popular misconception about human behavior that it follows all of the same rules that govern physical health. This so-called "medical model" of behavior suggests that when things go wrong it's because something bad, like a microbe or a virus, has attacked the patient and as soon as we can find out what it is and expose it to the purifying light of scrutiny, the sooner the patient will return to the robust good health that is a natural part of our genetic birthright. Psychologists even refer to problem behaviors as "symptoms," and look upon the magic cure as insight or understanding.

It reminds me of the fairy tale where the beautiful girl is freed of her tormentor's powers when she learns his name and calls him Rumpelstiltskin.

A problem in behavior is not a "thing." Bad behavior is not the surface manifestation of a demon hidden away inside a child that can be exorcised by words, it's not a virus that can be eliminated by a miracle drug, and it's very rarely the symptom of a psychological disturbance that traces its origin to some unfortunate event or relationship in the child's early life. Behavior, whether positive or negative, is simply the result of the consequences that attend a particular way of acting.

The belief that our behavior is caused by something in our minds that controls the way we act has been with us for a long time and has taken many forms.

In 1692 the citizens of Salem, Massachusetts, brought charges of witchcraft against several women, children, and men of the town. Many were tortured and some even executed to rid them of the demons that inhabited them and endangered the souls of the God-fearing. It was the behavior of the so-called witches that identified them to the "normal" people in the town.

Nine-year-old Elisabeth Parris suffered from fits and had been seen to throw a Bible across the room.

Her eleven-year-old cousin, Abigail Williams, tried to run up the chimney and threw firebrands around the house.

Other young girls in Salem began having fits and convulsions.

Clearly the devil, through the agency of a West Indian slave thought to be a witch, was controlling the girls, and soon hundreds of others in Salem, by possessing them with demons. The solution was to destroy the demons, a process which, unfortunately, destroyed some of the human beings as well.

Although the witch-hunting frenzy in Salem passed away, the belief in those demons has managed to survive, in different terms and in new guises. Today the demons are emotional problems, and while we nowadays don't burn the afflicted, we do rely on equally ineffectual and nonproductive (sometimes even destructive) ways of removing the demons. However, just as no one in Salem ever proved the existence of the devil except through the behavior of the witches and the possessed, so are today's demons elusive, except through the behavior that seems to indicate that they are lurking somewhere in the mind. Our form of exorcism is talking about the problem, in the belief that by identifying it and understanding it, it will go away. This procedure is almost as doubtful as burning witches.

Similarly, the trouble with the medical model is that it looks for root causes for problems that are nothing more than the wrong kinds of learned behavior. In the overwhelming majority of cases, a child's behavior is not written in the genes any more than it is dictated by the Devil—it's taught. There is an element of magic in the notion that finding the dragon in a child's psyche and naming it will cause it to lose its power and that the trouble will disappear. Some therapists have children pound clay, blow bubbles, draw pictures, and explore the "unconscious" by a variety of other means, all with the hope of illuminating elusive emotional problems that are nothing more than the results of having learned the wrong behaviors.

Looking for phantom emotional problems instead of amending those lessons costs money and wastes time. The real reward comes in changing feelings and behavior; just understanding them, as the EST people like to say, is the booby prize.

THE NEW EXORCISTS

"Our child was in therapy for years," parents sometimes tell me, "and I never knew what was going on. We saw so little change in all that time."

There are ways to help a child learn positive behavior, and some of the most effective ones are described in this book. But prevailing myths about raising children and about human behavior in general often go in the other direction. They create more problems than they solve, and sometimes send parents to ineffective sources of help in the vain hope of changing their children's behavior and feelings. Time and again I meet with parents who have had their children in psychotherapy for two or three years with little or no progress. In some instances, rather than improving, the behavior worsens.

At the beginning of psychotherapy, therapists often make a point of stressing that the process will take a long time. The inappropriate behavior has frequently been going on for years, they explain, and it will take years to understand and change it. Another common reason the therapy may take a long, long time, the parents are told, is that the child's "emotional disturbance" is so serious. It's essential to set up the expectation that therapy will take a long time because changes take place slowly, if at all; and the weekly visits by parents and child may continue for years. Without this expectation established at the outset of treatment, the parents at the end of the first year of therapy, seeing little or no progress, might seek help elsewhere.

When parents ask what is going on behind the doors of the therapist's office, they are told little—just enough to satisfy them. Indirect methods must be used, so they are advised, because the child is often reluctant to talk about problems. It is the rare child, in truth, who is verbal enough and willing to discuss with a therapist his or her innermost thoughts and feelings.

To get behind the child's resistance to talk (usually the lack of awareness that there's a problem to be uncovered), the therapist claims to be learning about the child's problems in more subtle ways—games, drawings, play activities. They're not games at all, the parents are told, but methods that enable the trained therapist to look within the inner recesses of the child's mind and help the child achieve insight into underlying problems.

Discussions of feelings and talk about problems don't appear to help a child learn positive, valuable behaviors even when the conversations take place between child and parents. If the person involved in such discussions is a therapist whom the child knows only through weekly visits, there's not even the bond of caring between them, and the discussions are even less effective.

A basic tenet of both child and adult psychotherapy is that people in treatment resist change because, on an unconscious level, they want to maintain the status quo. It's certainly a convenient concept. When I studied psychoanalytic theory a number of years ago, an analyst spent considerable time lecturing us about a number of his patients who had "failed" in therapy. As he viewed it, such patients had a need to hold onto the symptoms of their illness, and their resistance to therapy was more powerful than any treatment methods the analyst had at his disposal. I was impressed that the system was set up so that all the credit for success flowed in one direction and blame flowed only in the other.

The games and other activities the child therapist uses are meant to circumvent the resistance to change; in fact, anything the child does or says in treatment is grist for the mill—largely because the mill is bare, and there has to be something to talk about for two, three, or five years. Everything has "meaning" and can be related to the child as a person and is in some way related to his emotional problem. Pictures a child draws are analyzed for hidden meanings, games are viewed with this same eye to uncover secrets of the child's personality. Projective tests of questionable worth are supposed to suggest what is going on in the child's mind.

All the myths about dealing with children's problems and behavior at home are repeated in child psychotherapy.

"Let's talk about it . . ."

"Tell me what's troubling you."

"How do you feel about that?"

Since there is no research indicating that play therapy is effective, there is a good argument for methods that do help a child establish behavior we want to see or that help a child change problem behavior for the better in a comparatively short time.

Instead of going over and over and over the bad feelings and the bad behaviors, how much more sensible and productive to dwell on the good, however brief the moment, however expected the behavior, however often it occurs. This philosophy of raising children, of helping them solve behavioral difficulties, treats children as the unique individuals they are, responding to the values of their parents and their environment instead of to "demons" over which we have no control.

BEHAVIOR AS REINFORCED LEARNING

When we examine behavior, our usual concepts of cause and effect must be viewed from a new angle. Behavior is almost entirely a function of consequences—usually attention or the lack of it—that the child knows will follow immediately from a given type of action. For example, if a lollipop is used to stop a temper tantrum, based on that learning experience the child has every reason to expect a similar reward the next time—an assumption that ensures the tantrum will be repeated. Praise for a quiet behavior works the same way, only the effect is less noticeable than an angry tantrum. The quiet behavior will occur again as well—not in half an hour or a day or two, but eventually—if there is any expectation of the reward of praise.

Looking at behavior as reinforced learning is quite different from the way in which it is normally viewed, even by people who accept the concept of cause and effect. There is nothing to be gained from the kind of understanding that blames behavioral difficulties on situations over which there is little control: an unhappy relationship between mother and father; the fact that a mother must work outside the home; that one child requires more attention than another; or that there is some kind of "emotional disturbance" or "emotional disability." Unquestionably, the ways the members of a family relate to each other play a part in how a child behaves—but not because the relationships somehow implant the "demon." Rather, the behavior is a result of the ways such responses are rewarded or discouraged.

The child who learns to manipulate parents with antagonistic behaviors and to get attention for guilt-provoking statements such as "You don't love me," is not being driven by demons and/or despair. When these kinds of statements are habitual, they are a sign that the child is simply seeking—and apparently getting—a rewarding response: maximum attention from parents trying hard to acquit themselves of the false charges.

It is not always easy to resist the bait, but in matters of consequences for behavior, the parents cannot allow the child to control by way of guilt. While we do need to reassure children in their occasional moments of feeling unloved, parents must respond to the habitual use of attention-demanding behavior with minimum attention and time. This means no long discussion to find out why the child acted badly, but instead a clear message that the behavior is disapproved of.

Incidentally, it also isn't logical to attribute good behavior to pure chance (while demons often get the credit for bad behavior, no one suggests that angels are responsible for good behavior). If your child "turns out" well, it is because, consciously or unconsciously, you have given positive response—warmth, attention, affection—to positive behavior.

A child who becomes an accomplished piano player, eager to practice and achieve his or her best, doesn't just "happen" to be that way. Somewhere along the line, Mother or Father has given the right encouragement at the right time—immediate, positive consequences for good, piano-playing behavior. This is like the immediate consequences for early behavior that are so familiar we scarcely view them as similar: the smile and praise for the first word, the first step, the first of each of those actions a baby learns as it is growing up. The more positive responses an infant gets, the more likely these behaviors will occur again.

Your child's behavior, all through the early years, is very much in your hands. You need not seek for causes of behavior any further than the way you respond to the child and what you choose to encourage. You have the ability to teach your child the behaviors and feelings that reflect your values and the values you want your child to hold throughout life.

KAREN'S DEMON

Karen is an only child who has many behavioral problems. She would have a hard time in Salem today, let alone three hundred years ago. Her case is instructive, however, because it shows dramatically how different behaviors and their consequences relate to one another. It also shows how parents can take the most difficult situations and, through a step-by-step process, bring about changes for the better.

When Karen's mother sought professional help from me, she had already seen a variety of therapists who hadn't provided much concrete help in terms of changing Karen's behavior. The list of problems she presented was a long one.

Karen so decisively repulsed every child who ever tried to be her friend that she had no one left to play with. She was disobedient to her parents, and she argued just for the sake of disagreeing. She was nagging and persistent to get her own way. She told lies when it suited her, and, most hurtful to her parents, she frequently claimed that they didn't love her at all.

Karen's mother was deeply troubled both by her daughter's behavior and by the feelings she herself had about Karen.

"You notice she's there, you can't help doing that, and maybe she doesn't bother you at first," her mother said. "But she keeps on and on at you, and after a while you're ready to kill her."

The most common way to look at Karen's behavioral problems is, of course, to assume that she has an emotional problem, a demon that has taken hold in the mind of this seven-year-old and is controlling what she does.

"I thought I could find out what was causing all this trouble," her mother said. "I've tried to talk to her calmly and sensibly and explain why she shouldn't act this way, and then see if she couldn't tell me what was making her do it. I didn't get anyplace."

The mother expressed her thoughts about Karen's behavior in subjective terms, using abstract words that interpreted behavior rather than defining it concretely: lonely, sad, defiant, annoying, dishonest.

The first question that a parent has to answer in dealing with behavior, is: "Exactly what kind of behavior is represented by all those words?" For example, what does Karen do specifically that turns off other children? What does she do that you, the parent, find persistent and annoying?

"Friends?" her mother started. "Well, she doesn't have many, but when other kids are around she'll change the rules of the game to suit herself. I've seen her do that a lot. And she's bossy; she tells the others what to do, what games they're going to play. She argues with them, and her reaction to anything that doesn't please her is to get angry."

Karen's mother was specific about how Karen behaved around her: "Constant talking, anything that comes into her head; if I say white, she says black; nagging until I get so tired I usually give in and let her have her way."

The mother was seeking reasons for her daughter's behavior, and she was hard on herself in the process. There was a need to uncover and understand what was going on in Karen's head that made her such a difficult and clearly unhappy child.

"I've failed in my understanding of Karen," she said. "Her behavior has to mean something that I can't see, and someone has to help me find out what's troubling her, the psychological problem, and what is responsible for it."

The failure of understanding existed not in an inability to comprehend what was going on in Karen's mind but in what actually causes behavior—the mother's own response. When the mother began to express the nature of Karen's behavior in concrete terms, it became clearer to her specifically what she wanted for her daughter: the exact opposite of the way she presently behaved. She wanted Karen not to be bossy, not to disagree repeatedly, not to tell lies. In positive terms, she wanted her to be friendly, agreeable, honest.

How can Karen be taught to stop one kind of behavior and how can she be encouraged to behave in ways that produce positive results, that make people want to be with her, that will make her a happy child?

A major key to Karen's behavioral problems seemed to lie in her relationship with other children. No matter how badly she behaved, she was sure of getting attention from her parents. If she could learn to make friends with and keep as friends children of her own age, she would be earning the positive attention from them that she received from her parents following negative behaviors. That kind of result was sure to be a source of satisfaction that would provide a big boost in the direction of improving her behavior overall.

What I heard from Karen's mother was that she and Karen's father were putting a lot of energy, attention, and involvement into encouraging the wrong kind of behavior. They chided her for losing friends, talked with her about her behavior as though analyzing the obvious would change anything, argued with her—or allowed her to argue with them—endlessly. Karen was getting all the attention a child could want. It wasn't her fault that she didn't have any incentives to differentiate between attention for behavior that was good and behavior that was bad.

To lay Karen's demons to rest, her parents would have to supply those incentives—to find ways to encourage only positive behavior. My job as a psychologist was to teach them how to teach Karen new behaviors. If she had learned to behave badly because people paid attention when she did, she could learn to behave well for the same reason. The process is the same, whether you are a parent dealing with a single behavioral problem (as is usually the case) or simply trying to raise your children positively. The principle of behavior resulting from the response it gets holds true whether the behavior is terrible or terrific.

In Karen's case, her mother concentrated on helping make Karen a better friend, the opposite of the behavior that caused so much trouble for her. Karen's mother had to look at her with new eyes, which actually saw the occasional and fleeting instances of behavior that could draw other children to her. No child is wholly without such moments, and the challenge to the parent is to notice them and use them.

Karen's mother made a list for a week or two of examples of friend behavior. She was so accustomed to seeing only the things that troubled her about Karen that she had to make a real effort to see and remember the positive behaviors as they occurred. After a week, she had written down a handful of occasions, some of them very brief, that were positive, winning-friends behaviors. Karen's cousin—not a regular friend but a girl about the same age—came to visit. Karen let her go first in a game they were playing while the grown-ups talked.

Although Karen's other cousin, a baby boy, was probably too young to understand what she was saying, Karen told him how well he was learning to walk. She also picked up a toy he dropped.

A little girl from next door came by to play dress-up from a box of old clothes. Karen let her wear a big floppy hat that Karen usually claimed for herself.

The next step was to take those glimmers of positive behavior and make them important. The way to do it is through time and attention—and praise. Half an hour or more later, after the girl from next door had gone home, Karen's mother took her aside and talked about the incident, making it come to life again as vividly as possible.

"When Lucy was here this afternoon, and you were playing dress-up, you let her wear that big white hat you like so much. That was a nice thing to do. It makes me happy to see you share with Lucy. People like that in a friend."

Immediately and casually, Karen's mother followed her praise with ten minutes of doing something Karen enjoys, as if she had just thought of it: "Let's play a game of Chinese checkers." Suddenly, being nice to Lucy gets the same kind of attention being nasty to Lucy usually gets. Positive behavior has been made worthwhile.

The change in behavior comes when this process is repeated over and over again: a vivid description even an hour or more after the event, recreating what Karen did, who was there, what happened, what was said; praise from Mother for the behavior; several minutes of time spent doing something Karen enjoys.

The behavior of being nice to another child produces attention and praise from Mother. Being nice is worth repeating. (Using praise to encourage positive behavior is explored in greater detail in a later chapter.)

Karen's behavior in many areas began to improve with her parents' efforts to teach her new ways of acting. It became clear that "emotional problems" were not the source of her difficulties. There was no hypothetical demon controlling her behavior. That she began to make friends had nothing to do with talking about what was troubling her, but rather with her new behavior toward other children. And that she gradually stopped following her mother around with a constant stream of meaningless chatter, disagreeing with her or asking nagging questions, couldn't be traced to having uncovered deep resentments or insecurities but to the far simpler fact that Karen's mother no longer made it worthwhile for Karen to continue to do so. Instead of giving an agonized reply to a statement like "You don't love me," her mother chooses not to bite; she dismisses the remark with, "Karen, you know I love you." It sends a clear message: This kind of negative, attention-getting behavior is inappropriate—and it no longer works.

It takes determination on the parents' part not to give in to the temptation to explain, discuss, or analyze, when the child is touching sensitive areas. We want to be fair to the child and to ourselves, but it isn't necessary to hear Karen's side and to justify her parents' position, since this is what teaches Karen that interrupting, constant talking, and claiming Mother doesn't love her pay off.

"I spent a lot of time trying to understand something that wasn't even there," Karen's mother said after she had learned how to encourage Karen's appropriate behaviors and discourage her inappropriate ones. "It wasn't a 'problem' of the kind I'd imagined. There was no ailment that needed a miracle cure."

The problem was not an illness but a particular behavior, and it existed because of the way Karen's parents had always responded to it. When they learned to respond to other, less noticeable but more appropriate ways of acting—when they saw Karen with new eyes—they understood her behavior for what it was: something they were, with the best of intentions, teaching their child through nurture.

And when they applied that insight, the demons disappeared.

Chapter Four

THE UNDERSTANDING PARENT AND OTHER MYTHS

When a child is bleeding, the first goal of any rational intervention is to stop the flow. Nobody ever says, "Let's talk about it," and only a sadist suggests widening the wound. But a lot of people in my profession have been taught to nurture such childhood problem behaviors as emotional difficulties or attention deficit disorder, and in turn they teach parents to do the same thing.

For example, they teach parents to sit down with a child who has just sworn at them and ask, "What's bothering you? Are you upset because Daddy was insensitive or Mommy was too demanding?" When parents spend twenty or thirty minutes fumbling for the root cause while the swearing itself is ignored, they shouldn't be surprised when the offense is repeated. Parents who want to encourage appropriate behavior in a child have to demonstrate appropriate behavior themselves—and nurturing the wrong kind of behavior by giving the child a lot of undeserved attention is not appropriate.

I had a couple visit me regarding their six-year-old daughter because, they said, she was depressed. They then revealed that the little girl had many friends, adults loved her, and she did wonderfully in school. I asked how she could be depressed—it didn't make sense; depression is the absence of satisfaction in life, the result of everything going wrong and falling apart. But then I found out that both parents had been in psychotherapy, and the child had learned that every time she said she was sad or unhappy, they would sit down with her for twenty minutes trying to get to the source of the complaint. She didn't even have to be specific or give a reason—she had found magic words that would immediately trigger attention: "I'm unhappy." She was manipulating her parents with hollow words, and they rewarded the behavior with equally hollow responses.

"Let's talk about it."

"I want to know how you feel."

"Tell me what's troubling you."

"I'm trying to understand."

It's debatable whether an adult can really understand what's going on in a six-year-old's head, or that of a child who's seven or twelve or a teenager. It's even debatable whether there's any point in making the effort. Yet parents today are urged to try to "understand" their children, to look for hidden meanings in their words, to find out what's troubling them, to discover what they're thinking, how they feel about their parents, why they act the way they do, what makes them sad or defiant or happy. By entering into a dialogue with your child, the theory goes, you are getting close to the sources of behavior—the demons we talked about earlier.

CHILDREN NEED MORE THAN TALK

It would be fine for everyone if an exchange of words meant real understanding of behavior. It would be gratifying if an understanding parent were all that a child needed to be happy and well behaved. Unfortunately, today's elevation of understanding to the pinnacle of perfect parenting is a myth, engendered by the prevailing idea in psychoanalytic circles that talking about a problem solves it. This idea has put troubled individuals on thousands of analysts' couches for years of fruitless talking. So pervasive is this belief that parents assume that it will work with children, whether for a continuing behavioral problem or a solitary event.

When asked a question as simple as "Susie, why did you pick all of Mrs. Smith's tulips? Didn't you know it was wrong?" a normal child's answer is likely to be a mumbled "I don't know," followed by, "I just felt like it."

In attempting to understand and to help Susie understand, a well-meaning mother will frequently belabor the issue. She may interpret Susie's taking something that didn't belong to her as a sign of dishonesty or insecurity. If they don't work together to fully illuminate the mental processes that carried Susie over to Mrs. Smith's garden, Mother reasons, it will happen again—she'll start taking things from others. Never mind that "I don't know" is the simple truth. And never mind that a moment later, after Susie has thought about it as much as a child is reasonably able, "I just felt like it" is the truth as well. Let's just keep talking it over and over until we get to the bottom of this mystery of a child's character.

It may indeed happen again—not in spite of Mother's attempt for them both to understand, but because of it. Neither one of them will get any new insights about the incident by talking it over, but Susie is going to learn something else from their conversation about her relationship with her mother. The process is teaching Susie that she'll get all the attention she wants when she takes something from their neighbor's garden without permission. Of course, Susie isn't set on a path to habitual bad behavior by this one incident or by her mother's response. But if that response is habitual, there's a good chance it will increase the frequency of the behavior it unconsciously nurtures.

INADVERTENTLY REWARDING THE REFUSAL TO EAT

Understanding doesn't provide a solution to situations as simple as Susie's expedition among the tulips. And it doesn't help with those as anxiety-provoking as constant mealtime battles where children ignore the invitation to the table, refuse to eat, or demand certain kinds of food.

Unless a child is physically ill, there's no reason for the parent to try understanding—and tacitly excusing—a refusal to eat. But because the need to satisfy hunger is so basic, many adults see mealtime stubbornness as signifying a problem they have to understand; they're convinced their child's health and perhaps life depend on it. As a result, they mistakenly nurture the very behavior they're trying to discourage.

"Suppertimes are miserable," Andy's parents agreed. "He just won't eat, he claims not to like what is served, and then he sneaks snacks between meals or before bed. We've tried everything." They then listed for me the ways they nurtured Andy's not eating: ". . . giving him the things he asks for—and then won't eat—trying to persuade him, promising him treats if he will just finish the meal."

What's the mystery? Almost everything a child does from the very first cry says, "notice me." Is there some reason that fact of life should apply to everything but food? Look at how well it works.

Andy's father was quick to invent a far different scenario to explain this behavior. He told me he thought Andy was trying to punish his mother for some reason by not eating what she prepared. "The look on his face just seems to be saying he's getting even with us for something. We don't have any idea what we've done to make him feel this way. We've tried to talk to him about it, so we'll be able to understand him."

Seven-year-old Andy isn't about to help his parents understand. There is nothing to understand, except that he has learned to behave in this way at mealtimes (and he is not starving, because he has his snacks to rely on). And what he has learned—most likely because of inadvertent encouragement from his parents, a father who makes an issue of "cleaning up your plate," a mother who equates enjoyment of food with happiness—is that if he doesn't eat, he'll get a lot of attention from everyone around the table. That is all Andy's parents have to understand.

He's not trying to punish his mother; he's trying to bring her closer by drawing all her attention to himself by not eating. It isn't necessary to look further than the behavior itself and the consequences to understand what's happening and how to change it.

Andy's "problem" was solved not by understanding what was or wasn't going on in his mind but by giving him new responses to his behavior and nurturing new ways of behaving.

First, based on my advice to his parents, Andy was allowed to eat only at mealtimes, with no snacks available between meals or before bed. This gave him the choice of going hungry (unlikely) or eating with the rest of the family.

There were no more special menus; this was a home, not a restaurant, and meals were prepared according to the preferences of his mother and father.

When he refused to eat ("I don't like chicken," he said the first day, although chicken was generally something he asked to have made especially for him), nobody except his mother said anything: "That's the meal for tonight," she told him. No one pleaded with him to eat, or even asked him. The conversation went on around him and had nothing to do with his eating or failing to eat.

The first day, Andy didn't finish his meal within thirty minutes, and his mother wrapped the food and put it into the refrigerator.

"I am putting the food away," she said. "If you want it, you can ask me for it."

The first night was a hungry night for Andy. And it was a time without any attention.

The second night was a repetition of the first, except that he asked for his food a short while after dinner. He got it cold, without the reward of reheating or any other special treatment.

Andy wasn't the only one who began to change. By the time he got the message and started to eat at mealtimes, his parents were more readily accepting the notion that there had been nothing for them to understand in the first place. After a couple of days, the family's dinner-theater dramas came to an end. I told the parents that there was no need to take him aside and congratulate him on his performance at the dinner table; eating is a reward in itself, and doesn't need to be nurtured.

TOWARD GOOD TABLE MANNERS

Not all eating problems end as easily or as fast as Andy's did.

When the parents of five-year-old Paul complained to me that he stuffed food into his mouth or gulped it down so quickly they were afraid he might choke, I cautioned them to make a real effort not to lecture him on the virtues of good eating habits. Don't tell him not to stuff his mouth or to eat more slowly.

If a parent feels those behaviors cry out for some form of comment, be guided by the same rules that apply to any other form of criticism: make it brief and infrequent. The only legitimate purpose of such comment is to correct bad behavior, not to relieve a parent's anxiety and certainly not to continue a negative family tradition into yet another generation. Say something like "No, Paul," with a stern look on your face. *But again, if possible, say nothing.*

I told them that if a piece of food slips off Paul's plate, it shouldn't be the occasion for admonition or any other form of comment. You can't expect perfect table manners from a five-year-old. Repeatedly telling him what he is doing wrong at the dinner table will not improve his table manners. It will only associate eating with unpleasantness.

If Paul doesn't eat all the food on his plate, he shouldn't be forced to finish the meal—but he also shouldn't necessarily be rewarded with dessert. His parents can wrap the plate and put it in the refrigerator, and they shouldn't coax him to return to the table. Anytime before bed, Paul may ask for the meal he didn't finish, and he should be allowed to have it from the refrigerator, which is to say cold. If Paul actually finishes his meal but still wants something more to eat before bedtime, there's nothing wrong with offering him a snack, dessert, or sweet.

To encourage good eating habits, I advised the parents to take note of Paul when he is doing things at the dinner table that they would like to see more often: eating properly with his fork and spoon, eating more slowly, asking to have food passed, or eating even a small amount of a nonpreferred food.

I recommended they briefly tell him what he is doing at the time it is occurring. Comments such as "I am proud of you, you aren't stuffing your mouth" doesn't tell him what he is doing right, nor does a generalized compliment such as "You are eating so nicely." Tell him specifically what he is doing: "You are eating more slowly," "You are cutting your food so well," "You are using a napkin." Then *praise* him: "You are so grown-up. I am pleased with you."

After the meal, the parents should take Paul aside and tell him specifically what he did at mealtime that pleased them, choosing their words to bring the praised behavior alive again. They should immediately and casually follow the praise by spending several minutes with Paul doing something he likes to do.

LETTING IT ALL HANG OUT: THE PERILS OF FULL DISCLOSURE

A favorite myth, along with that of the understanding parent, is the idea that self-analysis and setting all your feelings free is good for you and good for your children. It's the modern equivalent to exorcism.

We often hear, "Let it all hang out," and, "say what you feel, and you'll get rid of all those bad feelings." While parents are being understanding about their children's problems, they're likely encouraging them to talk about why they're angry or depressed, in the real expectation that the children will become less angry, less depressed.

But that's just the opposite of how it really works. The child who's encouraged to talk about how angry or depressed he is will just get more angry, more depressed. A good test is to think back on times when you've been upset and have found yourself thinking and talking about it, telling whoever will listen all about it . . . and getting more and more upset and obsessive with each telling. It works the same way with children. Blowing off steam is one thing; I don't suggest that anyone hold back on expressing emotions—real anger, real sorrow, real happiness—either parent or child. You have a right to get angry, for example, when your child misbehaves. Children have strong feelings, too. What isn't right is encouraging them to talk about the reasons behind those feelings, over and over again, because you think that's going to help use up those feelings.

Consider this: If it's true that freely and endlessly expressing anger and depression uses them up and makes them go away, wouldn't the same be true of love and caring? Yet we don't have a finite amount of love that once spent, is gone for good. The more love you give, the more you have to give—and the more love you get back. By the same token, the more anger you use, the angrier you get. All of our emotions are subject to the same laws of economics.

"HAVE YOU HUGGED YOUR CHILD TODAY?"

Conversely, I have never recommended to any parent as a behavioral solution that they give their child more love. I have never told a Dad to spend more time with his son on a Sunday afternoon—take him to a baseball game or bond with him while fishing. I've never sent a mother and daughter to the flower show, and I never suggest that the bumper sticker we see everywhere—"Have you hugged your child today?"— is a prescription to cure anything. Certainly, I don't think any of those things do any harm, but I will never suggest that simply spending more time with a child or giving more love is going to resolve any behavioral problems. Yet the reminder to "give your child more love" is offered all too often as a solution to many childhood problems.

There is a whole spectrum of similar myths, the legacy of the same school of bumper-sticker psychology:

- A disruptive child will cease to be difficult if he or she "gets more love."

- An irresponsible child, a boy or girl who's dishonest, a child who's having trouble in school, a boy who has no friends, a girl who's selfish, all will start behaving well if they are hugged more often.

- All a child with problem behavior needs is more time with you.

All are fine sounding words, but without any real meaning when it comes to teaching behavior or changing it; they are myths that only mislead.

Love and hugging and time with a child are fine, but if you want to bring about changes in behavior, if you want to strengthen the bonds of affection between you and your child, you have to know *when* to give love and *how* to give it.

Don't make a show of being loving when a child demands it. The only thing a child learns from this is that demanding behavior brings verbal assurances that the child is loved—which encourages asking for love.

Loving your child should not be contingent upon *anything*. The time you spend with your child shouldn't be a bribe for better behavior. The manifestations of your love ought to be your spontaneous response to lovable behavior.

If, however, you are trying to solve behavioral problems, you can use that time and love in constructive ways. A child will not "repay" your love by changing his behavior just because you have reassured him of your caring. But he will learn new behavior if your caring is a consequence of positive behavior.

I once saw a mother who had taken her children to three different psychologists, and they all told her the children needed more love. "Had I brought my gerbils to the psychologists," she said, "I'm sure they would have told me *they* needed more love as well."

It's not a myth that children need love. The myth is in thinking it doesn't make any difference when and how the love is given. Giving a child more love or more time will not change negative behavior. In fact, if attention is given to a child following negative behaviors, it encourages more of the same. Love works just fine when it nurtures behaviors that build self-esteem. A show of love following negative behaviors will result in many more negative behaviors.

What parents may think they're doing at times like that is giving unconditional love, the kind that says, "I love you because you're you." That's seldom the message the child is receiving. Instead, the child learns that the parents come closer for negative behavior. In extreme cases, this response can encourage so many negative behaviors that the child becomes unlovable.

I once saw on the wall of a child guidance clinic: "Children need love when they least deserve it." If you follow this principle, the result will be more "least deserved it" behavior. Many therapists and parents are certain to interpret that slogan as a license to send a misbehaving child the wrong message. Giving children positive rewards for negative behavior is an inappropriate consequence, and it just leads to more of the same.

"Love conquers all" is one of the enduring myths of our civilization. The truth is somewhat more complicated. The bonds of caring and affection between parents and children are built up slowly as behavior and consequences make both parents and children more lovable and more loving.

"HONESTY IS THE BEST POLICY"
VS. NEGATIVE LABELS

Our ideas about feelings, letting it all hang out, and being honest about our emotions are somehow bound up with concepts about the therapeutic value of self-expression.

"Be honest." It's certainly a worthy goal. We do want our children to learn honesty, but there is nothing laudable about destructive venting, scapegoating, or negative labeling, honest or not. The result of being up front about everything, regardless of the pain it may cause others, seems to have little to do with the person you're being "honest" to, and a lot to do with what this honesty is supposed to do for you—it lets out the inner turmoil, the bad feelings will go away, you'll be a better person, all will be well.

But if we have to be so sensitive to the feelings of others, how do we convey hard truths to our children? The world out there isn't always going to praise. Very often it will criticize. Shouldn't we prepare our children for that, too—toughen them up, in a sense, for dealing effectively with life's inevitable adversities?

Say, for example, that you're playing tennis with your son. He's a beginner, and he's not very good at the game. You know that praise is what he wants, but his overall game has nothing praiseworthy about it. Can you praise him anyhow? Or should you tell him honestly how bad he is, in the hope that this will give him the incentive to try harder and perhaps help him be better able to face honest criticism from others?

There's the old saying "If you can't say anything good about someone, don't say anything at all." Like a lot of old sayings, it has some sense to it. Just because something is true, it doesn't have to be said, regardless of the current trend toward advocating total honesty. It's not going to do much for you or your child to tell him he's a terrible tennis player. Children believe what they hear about themselves. Praise for a good backhand stroke or a fast serve will mean something. He recognizes the truth of the praise; he can check the validity of your statement about his backhand with another player, a bystander, or the tennis pro.

The problem in recognizing the truth comes with the uncheckable, abstract statements a parent may make about a child. If you tell a child that a fire engine is a spoon, he will think you're being silly. He knows from his own experience that there is a difference between them; what you're saying isn't true. If you label a child with a personality trait, however honest and true you believe it to be, the child is out of the realm of fire engines and spoons and into something more difficult for him to make judgments about; abstract personality traits that aren't tied to concrete objects a child can recognize.

THE SHYNESS LABEL

Sam is quiet; he doesn't talk a lot when grown-ups are around. His mother defines this kind of behavior as "shy," and Sam frequently hears her saying, "Oh, Sam's the shy one. . . ." Maybe she even implies that shyness isn't a quality she admires; she'd rather have him be more outgoing like his brother.

Sam believes that he is shy. But who is to tell him what "shy" really means? Is it bad to be shy or is it possibly good? If his mother says he's shy, it must be true.

It would only make matters a lot worse if Sam's parents felt obliged to share with him the extensive clinical evidence that excessive shyness is one of those things, like blue eyes or big feet, that some of us are born with. Studies show that one child in every five or six is "behaviorally inhibited" from birth: reluctant to try new foods, apprehensive about new places or in the presence of strangers, generally uncomfortable with the unfamiliar. And if you're looking for a way to nail down the lid on a negative childhood trait, let him know it's not his fault about a child it's just the hand fate dealt him, that he was doomed to shyness from conception. And protect him from all the consequences of normal early life that could teach him confidence and encourage reaching out.

Never mind that without any outside help at all, a third of such "shy" children outgrow the trait by the time they're five. (Similarly, just because a child starts life with blue eyes is no guarantee they won't change color.) In his book, *Emotional Intelligence*, Daniel Goleman presents a persuasive case that shyness and natural timidity, while not among the most easily changed of all innate behavior patterns, are nevertheless responsive to relearning. Mothers, in particular, play a major role in encouraging or inhibiting children's creative responses to challenge, depending on whether they nurture boldness or deprive them of mastery of their fears by protecting them from everything. Either way, if you keep defining any child with labels, he's going to tailor his personality to fit the suit.

Comments about your child's self are about things no one can see: Janet is lazy, David acts like a baby, Sam is shy. It's not a question of fire engines and spoons any longer, things that are consistently given the same labels by everyone. Shyness, laziness, and babyishness are interpreted from behavior; not everyone will agree on them. The child cannot check on the validity of these assessments from another source, a grandmother, a friend, a brother or sister, because their definitions may be different. Rather, he will take his parents' words as truth: shy boy, lazy girl, dishonest, irresponsible, plain, or stupid. They become his way of thinking about himself.

Repeated criticism destroys a child's feelings of self-worth. Labels given by parents define his self-image. Honesty is not the best policy in the current meaning of the phrase, unless it is measured truth, given for positive behavior.

The fact is, honest praise that encourages feelings of self-worth is the one sure way to provide a child with a defense against the harsher criticisms of the world. A child with self-esteem knows he's worthwhile.

SETTING A GOOD EXAMPLE: DOES IT WORK?

We are told that if we set a good example for our children, they will follow in our footsteps. This is another myth with a particle of truth and not much more. Children do imitate adults, but setting a good example is not enough. Parents who set an excellent example in terms of responsibility may have children who are irresponsible and extremely dependent. Children from families who are gregarious and outgoing may be isolated and withdrawn. Parents, then, must do more than be good examples for their children. They must encourage behaviors they value, and this encouragement is perhaps more important than any example the parents represent.

This is not to say that children aren't influenced by parental example. The beginnings of behaviors are often inspired by parents and other influences around a child in his or her daily life—other children, teachers, relatives, television. Children very often imitate behavior they see, because, during the early years especially, they are eager to learn from the world around them and extremely accepting of what they see and hear.

Positive "imitated" behaviors must be encouraged, as should those apparently spontaneous moments of behavior we deem valuable: a thoughtful gesture, a step toward being grown-up, an interest in learning. They are delicate seeds of behavior that can be nurtured and helped to grow with the right kind of nourishment—praise and encouragement. They can, however, just as easily be discouraged by a failure to give them a boost.

With praise, behaviors will thrive, even if the parents themselves don't always set a good example. Your child can learn to be responsible and independent even if you at times are not a shining example. Parents who don't care about learning can have children who seek out knowledge—if the right kind of encouragement is there. Shy adults need not have withdrawn children, if they make an effort to provide sufficient encouragement for the child to make friends.

It all comes down to encouraging the kind of behavior that the parents value, whether it is opposite or identical to the way either parent behaves. What is important is that the significant people in a child's life look for valued behaviors and encourage them. The example you set is less a value or a detriment than how and what you encourage with your time, attention, and praise.

It sure beats talking about what went wrong.

Chapter Five

TEACHING AND LEARNING EMOTIONAL INTELLIGENCE

All parents are aware of their day-to-day responsibilities to their children: to see that they're fed and clothed and educated, kept from harm . . . and happy.

It's not difficult to understand what has to be done to take care of the physical necessities. We recognize dangers, we provide the food and clothing, we have school systems to undertake a good part of our children's education. But happiness? Who can define it, let alone say how to achieve it?

The happy child, as we've said, is one who is in touch with the many satisfactions life has to offer. The road to this happiness for both parents and children is simply one of teaching a child an appropriate behavioral repertoire, so that these satisfactions are more readily available. It's our responsibility as parents to teach children appropriate, emotionally intelligent behavior so that people want to be with them, and so that they are proud of themselves, learn to be grown-up, and, in turn, become responsible adults.

What is appropriate behavior?

It can be defined deductively: it's the opposite of the "wrong" behavior that everyone notices, the disruptive moments that get so much attention. Because we readily see all the things that are wrong, if we define a positive repertoire of behaviors, we have a menu for what we think the child should be doing.

Of course, that isn't all there is to it. Knowing what we want a child to do doesn't automatically yield a recipe for the necessary emotional intelligence to make it happen. Once the appropriate behaviors have been defined, we also need to develop a method for systematically nurturing the emotional growth required to change the direction of a child's behavior from a source of unhappiness to one of fulfillment.

SERMONS NO ONE HEARS

With a child who has problems, it's useful to examine the ways in which he learned his present behaviors before we set about teaching him new ones. There is nothing extraordinary about ten-year-old Doug: he's good to his younger sister, helps his parents, has lots of friends, and doesn't rock the boat at home. But he does have difficulties in school, and they're serious enough to cause his parents concern.

MOTHER: Doug's not stupid, we know that, but at school he simply has no motivation or a sense of the satisfaction he could get from doing well.

FATHER: The first time we heard anything about the problem was during a regular parents' night, from his teacher. She said he daydreams in class, he's completely disorganized, and he never seems to get his work done. Even though I was shocked, I immediately thought back to the last paper he brought home, and I recalled that I had seen right off that he'd done it just to get it out of the way. It was full of careless mistakes, things I know he knows are wrong.

MOTHER: He's slipshod about other things, too. Last week he left his brand-new jacket on the playground, and I can't tell you how many times he's lost his mittens or forgotten his coat. Of course, he's always forgetting his homework.

FATHER: We're both very achievement-oriented people, and we put a lot of commitment and energy into what we do. We'd like our kids to be that way, too. His younger sister doesn't seem to have the problems Doug has. She works hard at school, and although she's younger, we hoped he might start to look at her as the kind of good example he'd want to copy. But when she gets a perfect grade, even though he's obviously a little jealous of her success, it doesn't have the slightest effect on his own schoolwork.

MOTHER: We've had long talks with Doug about how important achievement is, but he scarcely listens. His father goes off to work every morning reminding him to try to do well that day, pay attention, do his best.

FATHER: Doug's a real good kid, except for this one thing. We don't want him to be held back, but the more we talk to him, the less he seems to listen. He's just as careless as ever, daydreams through the whole day. We've tried to set a good example for him, but that hasn't worked. What are we doing wrong?

That's a common enough question for parents like Doug's, who are highly motivated, with praiseworthy goals and an obvious concern for their son. They want him to be happy, they want him to do well, and they don't like the constant nagging and the family friction and unhappiness that are inevitable results of his apparent inattention and shirking.

What *are* they doing wrong?

They want very much to communicate their values to Doug, especially in the one area of school achievement. Their desire, however, is largely at the mercy of ineffective methods. It isn't necessary at this point to delve into what set of circumstances has made Doug behave the way he does at school. Sometimes even minor incidents can initiate negative behavior that demands attention and is repeated. By the time Doug's problem became what might be called chronic, the methods by which his parents chose to communicate their values were first, by modeling ("We're both very achievement-oriented. . . . We've tried to set a good example for him . . .") and second, by sermonizing ("We've had long talks . . . he scarcely listens.") A problem with sermons is that they contain implicit and sometimes overt criticism. Telling Doug "how important achievement is to us" is another way of saying he's not doing something that his parents value—usually followed up with telling him where he went astray.

To some extent, children do learn by example; that's the meaning of role modeling, and almost all of us start our lives by trying to imitate our parents. But in and of itself, communicating your values by example is often not very effective. The traditional child therapist who "sets a good example" for the child he is working with has to make the effort for many years before he sees his example take hold, if it ever does. Parents with the patience of a saint may hope that their example will give their children the inspiration to imitate them, and if they're lucky, it will. But in something as important as raising a child, we shouldn't rely on luck alone.

The other obvious way to communicate values is by words. But when you're faced with a behavior problem, those words tend to turn into sermons. A sermon, as we know, is a speech that attempts to make people mend their ways: "You are not living up to my expectations and I want you to change in a particular direction."

No one can prove that the sermons preached in houses of worship week after week for centuries or in revival meetings that repeat the same exhortations over and over again have any permanent and positive effect on the masses of people who are listening.

No one can prove (and many are the parents whose experience disproves it) that the sermons on good values and good behavior that parents give to their children have much effect on the young listeners.

Words from parents can send very powerful messages but not, I'm sorry to say, in support of the sermon's goals.

Part of the problem with sermonizing is that it seldom praises. Instead, a sermon generally says, "This is what you have done wrong, how you have not measured up, where you have failed; and this is how you have to change, to make amends." In communicating values to a child, it reads: "This is the behavior I am criticizing," and, "This is the way I want you to behave; this is valuable behavior."

Criticism is unpleasant. No one likes to be criticized, nobody is going to feel good about himself if he's frequently dealt negative comments. It hurts, and no one likes to be hurt, physically or verbally. Although people who attend church or revival meetings may be looking for a direction for their lives, it hurts nonetheless when they are told what they're doing wrong by a clergyman who supposedly speaks with the highest spiritual authority. The child who is given a sermon by his parents, who speak to him with the highest authority he knows, is likewise open to hurt by the criticism in their words. Is it any wonder that the words that follow, that tell him what he should be doing, fall on ears that are defended against hearing?

The natural response to criticism is anger, and then tuning out the message that's supposed to have a positive influence. The child can protect himself from the negative words of the criticism by becoming adversarial with his parents, perhaps attempting to enter a dialogue that justifies his behavior. (A mode not limited to kids; isn't your reaction to criticism by your peers frequently anger and/or an attempt to defend yourself?) Or he can simply tune out the unpleasant words and everything that follows them.

In order to protect himself from painful criticism, the child stops listening. The sermon has served the opposite effect of the one intended; not listening is incompatible with learning, so instead of amending inappropriate or nonproductive behavior, it entrenches it.

A child does not learn values by hearing them talked about in an admonitory speech following a pattern of criticism first, message last. Doug might well want to do better in school, but his tuned-out behavior to parents and teacher is not out of the ordinary. He's doing in his way what you or I would do under similar circumstances.

Sometimes parents will resort to various forms of punishment to help communicate values: say, sending a child to his room to think about his misdeeds for thirty minutes. Punishment, sparingly used, has some value in raising children, but I can think of very few boys and girls who will voluntarily subject themselves to thirty minutes (or thirty seconds) of painful reflection. They'll be thinking about something, but not what they did or how they're going to improve.

THE NURTURE RESPONSE

All this brings us to what method to use to teach values, and when. If you want to teach your child values, to help him learn more appropriate behavior, the wrong time to do it is after criticism. This is the nonteachable moment, when he will not be listening to you and won't learn a thing that's useful.

There is a right time, a time when the child is listening and open to learning from what you say. This is the teachable moment, a phrase that has been used before in different contexts but is a perfect description of the one time you can be certain that your words are going to be heard and absorbed.

The teachable moment, which is the key to teaching values and behavior, happens right after you praise a child for something he has done that pleases you, that represents a valued behavior you would like to see repeated and, more than repeated, become a part of his personality.

It is human nature to be a captive and attentive audience while you are hearing sincere words of praise that confirm that you actually are a worthwhile person. While a child may be listening to you at other times and is capable of learning from what you say, you can be certain of your impact only during the teachable moment.

In talking to Doug about his school behavior, his parents erect an insurmountable barrier of implicit or spoken criticism that prefaces the intended dialogue, and that barrier makes such moments almost valueless for getting across their ideas for how he might improve. Doug is turned off by these reminders of his failings, and anyhow he's heard it all before.

But the process doesn't have to begin with negatives. Certainly there are times when Doug does manage to get all his gloves, coats, and boots home, when he does produce a better than usual paper, when he demonstrates the very behavior his parents are trying to nurture into greater frequency. These occasions provide his parents with an ideal opportunity to make the positive behaviors worth repeating. If Doug is praised for these desired but regrettably rare occurrences, they can be sure he'll be tuned in, not tuned out, and every word will register with maximum impact. Praise sounds good, and in that context whatever else his parents have to say about their values won't pass unheeded: the importance of achievement, how responsible it is for him to take care of his clothes, how grown-up he is to do his schoolwork promptly and well.

In the teachable moment, Doug's mother and father can communicate the values they feel are important. Although we have a general consensus about what is good behavior and what is not and what values are significant, it truly is in the hands of parents to nurture the qualities they personally wish to see in their children. Any parent can learn to communicate values purposefully, instead of at random, simply by knowing when a child will be most receptive. They can teach appropriate behaviors, help a child learn positive behavior, and encourage feelings of self-esteem so essential to the creation of a happy human being.

The teachable moment is a critical time, and parents have to make a conscious, consistent effort to learn to use it. Of course, this isn't an unfamiliar idea to many parents. We all know people who have no trouble choosing just the right moment for spontaneous praise, and it seems that they naturally follow the methods that I teach parents. It is likely that their own upbringing has taught them to see and respond to the quiet moments of behavior we wish to encourage. But anyone can do it, whether they want to change unacceptable behavior or nurture positive behaviors until they are strong enough to stand on their own.

COMMUNICATING VALUES

The sequence for communicating values to a child is as easy as ABCD, and is so simple that it quickly becomes a natural way of relating to your children. Start with a new awareness, and learn to look at your children with new eyes. Seek the quiet but positive moments of behavior you wish to encourage. Then, from thirty minutes to several hours later, and at your convenience . . .

A. Take your child aside, in private, and make the earlier behavior come to life again by describing it in words. Make the behavior so vivid that as you are telling about it your child can picture it in his/her mind's eye.

B. Then immediately follow this with 100 percent praise. Do not say, "It's nice to see that you're not hitting your brother for a change." Tell your child that he has done something that pleases you, that he has behaved in a way that is well thought of, not only by you but by his friends and the people in the world outside the home. And praise him specifically. Knowing *how* to praise is as important as knowing *when* to praise (two dimensions to be discussed in more detail in the next two chapters.) In this sequence, praise gives you the undivided attention of your child.

C. Then immediately tell him/her why this behavior is of value. "You were being a good friend," or "People like that in a friend," or, "That was grown-up, mature, more adult, like a big boy or a big girl."

D. Immediately—and casually —follow this with between five and fifteen minutes doing something your child enjoys. Spending enjoyable time together is an effective added investment in worthwhile behavior that confirms the praise and associates it in the child's mind with another positive event. It's not a bribe—"If you do this, I'll do that for you"—but a form of attention that follows valued behavior. This kind of positive reinforcement is far more beneficial than attention given, say, for refusing to eat or throwing a tantrum, or any one of the many other disruptive behaviors that engage parents and often lead them down a dead-end path of trying to understand what is going on in the child's head.

This ABCD sequence can be applied to communicate values and teach behavior in just about every situation in raising a child. It's a positive way to help a child learn behavior and, unlike the extended periods of time required for traditional child therapy, it is an amazingly rapid way to change behaviors and feelings—even those that have been entrenched for years. Best of all, it is entirely in the parents' hands. They set the goals they want to achieve. They make the judgment about which behavior they think is valuable and which is without value or of lesser value. The decisions are not made by a third party, a therapist or an adviser on parenting, but by the people who are most interested in having the child grow up according to their system of values and behavior.

Children, like anyone else, want to feel good about themselves. They quickly begin to behave in ways that bring them praise and the warmth, attention, and caring so essential to a sense of fulfillment, self-worth, and true emotional intelligence. All you have to do to start them on the right road is catch the appropriate moment and make it meaningful with praise. Each such nurturing of valued behaviors is a small but significant step toward a happy, productive life.

Chapter Six

WRITING IN YOUR CHILD'S BOOK OF LIFE

Modern neurology tells us that our memories endure as long as we do, and they influence the ways we act long after our imperfect retrieval systems have eroded and we have lost the ability to recover details or even whole events. Similarly, everything that happens to children is written in their memories, and it stays there through the end of their lives.

Fifty years from now, Hannah won't be able to recall details of all the affirming or discouraging moments that fill her sixth or seventh years. She won't remember every conversation with her parents, every "You're wonderful!" or each "How could you?" But a big part of the way she feels about herself on the last day of her life and all the days between is printed by her parents in her childhood. Hannah's book of life, like each of our own, is a history less of events than of signals she has received regarding the kind of person her parents and others have decided her. More than a ledger of assets and liabilities, it has a plot that will turn on how, at six and at sixty-six, Hannah reads her balance sheet.

That is the reason, in all of a parent's transactions with a child, it's impossible to overstate the power of appropriate praise; it gives the child a positive attitude toward him- or herself that can shape his or her entire life.

We have talked about when to praise, when to communicate to your child that behavior is valued. Now let's consider how.

"I AM A WORTHWHILE PERSON"

I often come across adults who look upon life as a repeated series of examinations. Their daily life is a never-ending attempt to prove their worth, and it's an attempt that's doomed to failure. Although these feelings may spur them on to success in business, academic, and social situations, no accomplishment seems to increase their feelings of self-worth. The success that's achieved is reached at a very high cost: constant tension, never being able to relax because life is an unceasing struggle to affirm that they're really doing a good job, that they're worthy.

Others may lack even this driving urge to succeed. They downgrade all their accomplishments, nothing is "good enough." It is as if such people are saying to themselves, "Whatever I do is worthless because it is what I have done, and I am a worthless human being." It's like the old Groucho Marx joke about answering an invitation to join the Friars Club; Groucho said he had doubts about whether he should belong to any club that was willing to accept him as a member.

What we see in adults is a way of thinking about the self that has its roots in childhood. If no one helps the child establish the basis for self-esteem, if he's never praised and always criticized, he's going to have some serious doubts about his feelings of self-worth. And as that child grows into adulthood, things won't improve; he still isn't going to have positive feelings of self-worth.

Parents have a unique opportunity to encourage positive feelings of self-worth in their children. Their words have enormous impact. Giving a child this sense of self-esteem may be the most important responsibility parents have, if they want a happy child and if they want the child to become a happy adult.

Specific praise—tied to even small events a child remembers and to the behaviors we want to encourage—builds self-esteem and adds to the asset column on the balance sheet. Each time a child finds himself in a similar situation, he knows a little more about what types of behavior are appropriate, what will earn him further rewards of praise and success.

Eventually, what parents see and praise in these small quiet moments will become the child's customary behavior—a quality of his personality. These traits, their manifestations in the way the child behaves, are what others in the world see and think are worthy of their praise as well.

By that appropriate praise, when you compliment a child on being polite or thoughtful, for being grown-up or a good friend, you are offering something that has an effect far more important than just making the child feel good for the moment. Little by little, the words of praise given by parents become part of the way the child thinks about himself or herself as a person:

> Others like what I have done; maybe I ought to like myself, too. Maybe I am worthy of my mother's or father's words of praise. Yes, I am worthy.
>
> I do like myself.
>
> I am competent, grown-up, responsible.
>
> I know what I'm doing, and I'm doing a good job.
>
> I am a worthwhile person.

In times to come, even when praise is less frequent from an often indifferent world, the feeling of worthwhileness is always there.

AVOID DEVALUATING PRAISE

If you acknowledge a positive behavior with praise, which is one of the most powerful rewards available to a child or adult, the nurtured behavior will occur more often. However, you don't want to overdo praise to the point that you devalue the gift. Indiscriminate praise reduces the worth of praise that has been earned, and excessive praise discourages a child's internalization of feelings of self-esteem by causing an overdependence on external words of approval. You're preparing the child for a world in which praise is not given repeatedly for all things that are praiseworthy, and a world that looks upon too much praise as insincere. If you praise effectively to build a solid base of self-esteem, constant praise is unnecessary.

Parents may also mistakenly praise the wrong things. Sonia is eight, and nobody would call her a badly behaved child. She's quiet and polite and goes about her business without ever rocking the boat. Her parents have never had to or wanted to criticize her. Yet Sonia has doubts about her worth as a person. She never feels that she's competent, she doesn't really think she ought to like herself. Sonia is a child who is often praised inappropriately, not just for positive behaviors but for nonbehavior.

"You're such a good girl, you're so quiet, I didn't even know you were there."

"Quiet as a mouse . . . good as gold."

Sonia is praised for doing nothing, and her parents think of her as a "good" child. That she is, but nurturing passivity encourages her to go through life unsure that she's worth anything except when she's not doing anything at all. When parents don't say they like what she's done any better than what she hasn't done, when they equate habits of nonbehavior and good behavior, they risk imprinting that message.

In little girls especially, quiet behavior is traditionally seen as "good" behavior, whereas physical boisterousness can be considered more commonplace in boys. We expect boys to get involved more frequently in situations that create momentary havoc, but because that "bad" behavior is within cultural norms, they receive fewer incentives to passivity or nonaction.

Chuck discovers that it's fun to throw stones, and then something gets broken. That doesn't get Chuck praise from Mother or Father. It gets him a talking to, at the very least. It probably doesn't stop Chuck from throwing stones.

How different it might be, though, if Mother or Father took the fact that Chuck is learning to throw well, praised it as a sign of a grown-up ability, then suggested that he'd get far more satisfaction from throwing a ball than a rock—why not use that throwing skill with a baseball or football instead?

Instead of thinking, "I'm a bad kid because I throw stones and break things," Chuck will think, "I'm competent, I'm good at throwing a ball, my parents praise me . . . and I'm worthy of that praise."

Building self-esteem in children creates a process and a map, giving them the nurture to take their own worth for granted and providing direction for getting a similar reward habitually through life. Meanwhile, they needn't waste energy and lose momentum with feelings of self-doubt, but will be able to use their energy to work toward productive goals. The book of life that has a happy start will probably stay happy through to the final chapter.

HOW DO WE KNOW PRAISE WORKS?

The process of praise and building self-esteem and the appropriate behaviors in our children is not necessarily a swift one, and a word of praise won't always alter behavior immediately. Encouragement of quiet behaviors as the child shows them from very early years often has the same action as a time-release cold pill, except it extends much further out in time.

As a psychologist who has taught parents how to use this method with their children, I can be confident of the long-term result because of the times I've seen it happen. Parents must have some of that same confidence that a process is taking place in which some of the results are not immediate, especially when they include such qualities as maturity and kindness and responsibility.

It does work.

Think back to the time your child said his first word. "Mama . . ." It was probably a major moment in your life.

You encouraged your child to, "Say it again, say 'Mama' . . ." And say it for Father, for Grandma, for aunts, uncles, neighbors. You reward those precious first words with attention and, implied in the attention, praise.

How about baby's first steps? More praise. The same for any of the other milestones that mark the transition from helpless infant to child. Encouragement of one word leads to saying more words. Encouragement of the first step leads to an effort to take more steps—in spite of spills and bumped noses.

But what about other achievements, less concrete ones, that are also part of growing up? Unfortunately, we don't pay similar attention to the flowering of less obvious skills for living: kindness and caring, honesty, a sense of humor, a sensitivity to others, all the things we're really talking about when we examine what we mean by a happy child. Yet if we see that learning to walk and talk, or learning to tie shoes and eat properly can be encouraged by praise and attention, why not the other skills, even if occasions necessitating, say, honesty don't happen as often and as regularly as the necessity for speaking or tying one's shoes?

They can, and habits of character should be rewarded with the same notice and nurture a parent gives to any milestone.

OPENING NEW CHAPTERS

In thinking about the kinds of behavior you want to nurture in your child, you're probably going to come up with the same categories as most other parents, and you may even give those categories some of the same names. *Sibling caring*, and *thirst for learning* are two common ones. A couple of other names I've found useful are *Mother Theresa behaviors*, and *taking disappointment calmly*. Here are some illustrations of how they work.

Taking Disappointment Calmly

Jane's favorite television show is changed to a new hour, past her bedtime. Without complaint, she accepts that she can no longer watch it.

A clothing crisis arises when Sarah is getting dressed for school: she can't find her favorite shoes. After an appropriate effort by both Sarah and her mother to find the shoes, the little girl says, "That's okay, Mommy; we'll find them tonight when I get home, and I'll wear them tomorrow instead."

Bill asks his mother if a friend can come for dinner that evening, and she says no because it's a school night. He says, "Oh," and goes on with his activity.

Although Mary has played all day with her friend, it's obvious she's disappointed the fun is ending when her mother comes to pick her up. Even so, she stops playing, puts on her coat, and says to her friend, "I had a lot of fun today; I'll see you tomorrow."

Sibling Caring

Kelly tiptoes into her baby sister Samantha's room, and when she sees Samantha is awake, Kelly starts to sing songs to her.

Jimmy reads a story to his little brother.

May asks Mommy to buy a second ice cream cone so her little sister can share in their treat.

Charlie wants to play cowboys, but he good-naturedly agrees to a different game when his older sister suggests it.

Mother Theresa Behaviors

Johnny is already late to the baseball game, but he asks his mother to take the time to pick up a friend who doesn't have a ride.

Betty invites the new girl home from school "because she just moved here and doesn't have any friends yet."

When Harold gets up from the dinner table, he carries his plate to the sink.

Georgia turns down the television set when Mother is using the telephone.

Jack picks flowers for his mother on the way home from school.

Thirst for Learning

The twins make a game of sighting different states' license plates on a family trip.

Angela and Ruth have a spelling bee.

Freddie reads through his father's newspaper every afternoon when he gets home from school.

As I see it, parents are the gardeners in their children's garden of behaviors, and they have to select and nurture those behaviors that are the basis for self-esteem, happiness, and the character traits they want their children to have as adults. This process is called parent selection.

INSTINCTS AND PARENTS

Talking and walking, you might be saying, are instinctive. They are. The human abilities to walk upright and to make sounds that express our thoughts are born in us and flower with the nourishment of encouragement and example. But there are instincts and "instincts," and parents today have been confused by what is called "following your instincts" in raising children. Too many advisers on raising children suggest that whatever you do as a parent is okay; the chances are good that "instinctively" you'll do the right thing. This may help you get to sleep at night, but you can't count on it. Some of the most important parts of parenting don't work that way at all.

Of course we have instincts, not only our means of moving and the way we use our vocal cords, but also instincts for food, for sex, for activity. It's the variety of choices about how those instincts will be satisfied that distinguishes us from ants and bees, who move, make sounds, eat, reproduce, and go about their business within an extremely limited range. A bee from the East Coast of the United States, for example, will behave in pretty much the same way as a bee from the West Coast, but a child born in America and raised in China is not going to be the same child she would have been had she remained at home. Her instincts will be the same, but her ways of satisfying them will be different. Most behavior in human beings isn't imprinted in the genes, the way it is with ants and bees.

The process of childhood development owes more to what I call "parent selection" than to natural selection. Parents cannot simply follow whatever impulses seem the strongest at the moment; they have to use their brains, to deliberately and consistently select those behaviors that are consistent with the values they want to encourage in their child through the nurture response.

"PARENTAL INSTINCTS" ARE ACQUIRED

The concept of a universal parental instinct is a fallacy. Parents who "follow their instincts" aren't responding to some deep impulse common to all people; they're answering to aspects of their own behavioral repertoire learned from their parents. This is neither good nor bad, but it does take away some of the glamour surrounding the mystique of following our instincts. The instincts in question are actually ways of behaving that were acquired—the way we acquired food preferences, attitudes about religion, politics, men and women—from the people who raised us.

You may not be the kind of person, for example, who learned to praise spontaneously, but you can make a conscious effort to do so now, even if it runs counter to your so-called instincts: in other words, what you learned in the past. If, on the other hand, you are a parent who does seem to have an "instinctive" ability to see and understand what ought to be praised, you are probably also a person who experienced praise as a child.

The "instinct" for praise is, happily, something we can acquire. This brings us back to learning to see our children with new eyes—and responding to what we see, however small, quiet, or expected it may be, with encouragement and the knowledge that our words are going to have a profound effect on their behaviors.

SELECTION/REJECTION: CAN LOVE MAKE A CHILD UNLOVABLE?

For good or bad, Darwin's theory of natural selection doesn't apply to children's behavior. The fittest behavior doesn't necessarily survive while the least appropriately adaptive behavior withers on the vine. Parents must do the selecting and rejecting when it comes to raising children, to choose the behaviors they want to survive and those they'd like to see fade away. In child rearing, the way natural selection really works is not through a child's genetic legacy, but through the things parents say to their children—the ways they present and nurture their own values.

One problem with that method is that adult belief systems are often extremely negative and potentially harmful. Consider the common case of the mother who is herself the product of an abusive upbringing, who was called stupid, irresponsible, dishonest, or ugly as a child. In trying to be the parent she wanted for herself, instead of being an abusive mother, she becomes overly permissive. It's easy to imagine her saying to herself as a child, "When I grow up, I'm going to be just the opposite of my own mother; I'm going to be the mother I wish I had." And in fulfilling that ambition, by nurturing behaviors that need to be discouraged, she creates a monster.

That's pretty much what had happened to Helen Keller, before Annie Sullivan arrived on the scene. There was no abuse, but her parents felt sorry for her and they nurtured behaviors that eventually were completely out of control. With or without abuse in their own backgrounds, many parents nurture out-of-control behaviors because they want to become the parents they never had, and as a result they have difficulty setting appropriate limits.

I recall one client who came to motherhood with that background, and her own daughter was completely out of control. Every time the child did something outrageous, instead of responding with appropriate consequences, she would sit down and attempt to reason her back to acceptable behavior. There were times when the mother became so frustrated she would yell at the child in anger. But even that didn't help them to break the circle; after an hour or two of examining her own actions under the lens of remembered childhood pain, the mother would skulk back to the daughter and beg for her forgiveness.

What the mother and the child both needed to know was that Mommy's yelling meant nothing more than that she had reached her limit, and this was a natural result of the child having done everything possible to provoke her.

When maladaptive ways of responding to children are a function of these early belief systems, "following your instincts" is a chancy route to making the right kind of selections. What isn't rejected may well end up as the problem behavior that brings parents to child psychologists.

There are fairly common ideas of "right" and "wrong" behavior—especially the latter, because it tends to disturb the waters in an obvious way. You're pretty quickly made aware that Doug isn't doing well in school, that Karen doesn't have any friends, that Chuck throws stones, that your son tells lies or your daughter is always a problem at mealtimes. If it's a question of black and white, you don't have trouble recognizing it, and the problem may just be finding a way to correct what's wrong and nurture what's right.

Selection and rejection are somewhat more difficult in the gray areas—which also happen to be the areas where "instincts" are most likely to go wrong.

We want our children to be happy. We want what's best for them. We want to give them what we think will bring them fulfillment. Like adults, children use things as a measure of happiness, and many are the parents who succumb to requests for this toy seen on television, that kind of candy, all in the name of wanting to make their children happy. A reliance on material goods, however, merely shows how easily we are confused in the impulse to give the gift that counts. A nearly exclusive reliance on that kind of reward to a child, even with the best of intentions, is the least likely road to happiness.

There are lots of ways in which we can do too much for our children. The South Seas idyll, the dream of Eden, where food falls from the trees in a benevolent climate, where no effort is necessary to survive, is a delusion. And that view of paradise doesn't graft easily with the comforts of a technological society and the "good life" as exemplified by Western culture. The concept of something for nothing can cause cultural dislocations that aren't quickly remedied. It can cause unhappiness.

In William Gibson's play *The Miracle Worker*, Annie Sullivan encounters the wild and unmanageable Helen Keller and her mother. Mrs. Keller says, "Like a lost lamb in the parable, I love her all the more." Annie, whose task it is to teach Helen, says, "Mrs. Keller, I don't think Helen's worst handicap is deafness or blindness; I think it is your love and pity.... All of you here are so sorry for her, you've kept her like a pet. Why, even a dog you housebreak..."

The wrong kind of love can make a child unlovable. Love doesn't always mean permission, and it doesn't always mean reward. It's the wrong kind of love when we say yes on "instinct"—because it's easy and makes us feel good for a moment—when instead we should be saying no.

Chapter Seven

HOW TO PRAISE, WHEN TO PRAISE, WHAT TO PRAISE

Parents praise their children naturally. We hardly think about it, although we do know that praise is good—and for most people, easy. Parental praise builds self-esteem in a child, the quiet inner feeling of competence that helps determine success in life.

We shouldn't, however, find it necessary to praise our children constantly. In fact, as I have already said, if we praise too much we will discourage the development of what might be called "self-praise," the child's ability to know without being told that he is doing well, and we will encourage overdependence on external words of approval.

Early on, every child needs words of praise, sincere approval, and nurture for ordinary behaviors. It isn't long before that need reduces, however, and we must attempt to prepare the child for a world in which praise is not given repeatedly for all things that are praiseworthy. Most children will interpret too frequent parental praise as insincere or even manipulative as they grow to realize that pats on the back don't occur all that often elsewhere.

WHAT IS YOUR PRAISE REALLY SAYING?

We've examined the role of praise in the teachable moment that follows words of praise to communicate values or teach behavior. But simply telling a parent to praise a child is like a doctor telling a sick person to take some medicine without specifying the name, the dosage, or the length of time it should be taken. Medicine, like praise, sounds good, but without a few instructions, both prescriptions are equally worthless and potentially harmful.

The recipe for giving praise to encourage appropriate behaviors is simple:

- Be specific.
- Give 100 percent praise.

"You were very good" doesn't tell a child much, although it's clearly praise. "You were very good when you helped your brother read that story. That's being thoughtful and grown-up; I like to see that" tells the child exactly what he's done and why it pleases you.

Often what parents think of as praise is in reality loaded with implied criticism, things they would never say if they remembered to be specific and wholehearted about the behavior they're trying to encourage. Since parents normally pay most attention to behavior that rocks the boat, when a child does behave well "for a change" it's behavior viewed in comparison to what is usual. Unless a parent is careful and deliberate, it's very easy to succumb to a pattern of offering praise for those brief moments of quiet, positive behavior in exactly the wrong terms—in language loaded with subtle criticism. When the spoken words are praise but there's another meaning underlying them, children are quick to pick up the second message. The praise is valueless unless it is complete praise, tied to the specific behavior you want to encourage.

Here are some examples of praise that are really criticisms and how the good behavior might have been better nurtured.

Non-praise: "You played very nicely this afternoon for a change."

MEANING: I didn't notice what you did that was so nice, I'm just happy you didn't fight and argue the way you usually do.

"Playing nicely" doesn't say much to a child, and "for a change" isn't praise at all, but an implied criticism of usual behavior. The comment offers the child no incentive to repeat what was "nice," and basically what he's been told is that what pleases his parent is his not getting the customary negative attention.

Real praise: "You played very nicely this afternoon. I liked the way you showed Jeff how to glue the new model airplane together and then paint it. People like friends who are helpful."

Non-praise: "It's about time you picked up your room."

MEANING: You never pick up your room when I ask you to, and it always annoys me. You did it this time, but it probably won't happen again.

It's not praise if it comments only on the fact that the child has obeyed a request, especially when it doesn't give any reason for the value of doing a chore or what purpose it serves other than getting something done that the parent thinks is necessary. And the implied criticism ("It's about time . . .") means that it probably won't happen again soon, either.

Real praise: "You picked up your room. It looks terrific. I like the way you put all your toys together in one place. It pleases me to see you putting your things in order like this."

Non-praise: "You have four A's and a B on your report card. That's good, but we've got to get that B up there."

MEANING: Those four A's are good, but they're not good enough for me. You won't really measure up in my eyes until you get straight A's.

Praise that's contingent upon perfection is without value. No one is perfect, and in spite of some parents' belief that holding up ultimate goals will make a child try harder, it simply confirms the suggestion that she'll never be good enough, no matter what she does.

Real praise: "I'm so proud of you for getting such terrific marks on your report card. Wow—four A's!"

———

Non-praise: "I'm glad to see you sharing with your brother. What a shock!"

MEANING: You're a selfish person. It's about time you began sharing.

Children, as has been discussed, believe what they're told about themselves. If you suggest negative qualities, the child will begin to think of himself that way. Tell a child he's self-ish often enough, directly or under the guise of "praise," and he's going to believe he is selfish. "That's what they tell me. They must know."

Real praise: "I like to see you sharing with your brother. It was very nice of you to let him ride your bicycle this afternoon."

———

Non-praise: "It's nice to see you're not acting silly."

MEANING: You usually act silly. For once you aren't. I haven't bothered to notice what you're doing well, but it's not im-portant, as long as it's not silly.

This kind of comment is so nonspecific, talking about what a child didn't do, that it can't be called a positive reac-tion to behavior. And since no one bothers to define what "not silly" is, it's difficult for a child to know what ought to be done to earn parents' praise and, more important, why that behavior is valued.

Real praise: "I was happy to see that you acted in a grown-up way today. You said 'Please' and 'Thank you' to the people who were visiting. I was very pleased."

Praise only works when it sends a specific, positive message: I saw what you did; I was interested in the things that you did, interested enough to take note of exactly what they were; what you did pleased me; what you did is valued behavior.

WHEN VIRTUE IS NOT ITS OWN REWARD

I have encountered parents who feel that praise isn't good for a child, or that it's something meant only for very young children. They feel that a child should behave well without encouragement; it's difficult for them to praise, even when it's explained how the system of praise and the teachable moment work. They deprive their child of vital parental nurture when they suggest instead that "virtue is its own reward."

This may be a laudable philosophy, but it lacks validity in terms of raising children, if you understand that behaviors, good and bad, are learned as the child grows up and do not spring from inborn sources within the mind. Neither demons nor angels but encouragement in the form of time and attention for certain kinds of behavior is going to determine how your child acts.

Children need to have someone be proud of them before they can develop feelings of self-worth. It's no virtue to behave well in your young years if the behavior is little more than a happy accident and you really don't know what virtue is all about. The "reward" for virtue happens when reinforcing words of external praise gradually become internalized in a character pattern of cause and effect—"I am a worthwhile person."

"But I don't know how to praise," one mother said. "Even when Kevin does something well, and I know it, it sounds fake when I praise him. Maybe it has to do with the way my childhood was. I was never praised."

This same mother admitted that she never really thought much of herself, and agreed that it was worth making the effort to praise Kevin if it would increase his feelings of self-worth. Kevin had been having trouble getting along with other children, and the praise was intended to encourage new winning-friends behaviors.

"It works," she said later. "Kevin's a changed boy." She thought for a moment, then added, "I've changed, too. It's not so hard for me to see the good things he does and to say how much I like to see him behaving that way. I even find myself doing it with his two sisters, who don't have behavior problems, but they really look pleased when I give them a little pat on the back."

HOW MUCH OF A GOOD THING IS ENOUGH?

Another common belief among parents is that praise simply isn't good for a child, that it will lead to bad behavior rather than good.

"If I say something good, something bad is sure to happen," a parent reasons. "So to be safe, I won't say anything at all."

Or: "It's okay to criticize, because things couldn't get worse, and a few hard-hitting words might help make them get better."

In the the first case, the "Let sleeping dogs lie" myth is close to the idea of praising nonbehavior discussed earlier. It's also related to the idea held by some people that anything good has to be paid for, that there's no pleasure without pain. But it's false that withholding praise has no effect. A child who is not praised has no guidelines for what his parents think is valuable.

In the second case, the idea that criticism is helpful in improving a child's behavior is probably a harmful way to teach him anything. If praise helps a child develop a positive image of himself as capable and worthwhile, with a strong ability to praise himself, repeated criticism does precisely the opposite; it creates a negative self-image. The words of criticism become the language heard within, an affirmation of worthlessness.

Nine-year-old Howie invariably looked at himself negatively. He was well behaved, his parents said, but his poor self-image was clear in the things he said about himself:

"Nothing ever turns out right for me."

"Every time I try to do something, I goof up."

Increasingly, Howie was reluctant to get involved in activities where success wasn't guaranteed. (For example, he took part in the school track program because he was a better runner than many older boys; he didn't swim willingly, "because the other kids are too good for me.")

"He watches television all the time, he won't take any initiative," his parents said.

You can't fail if you're watching television; you can't fail if you're passive.

"We try to encourage him to go out and try," his father said. "We do praise him, but it doesn't do any good."

Part of Howie's problem, it turned out, was not only that his negative statements about himself were related to an ideal of success that meant doing things perfectly, but his self-deprecating comments were subtly reinforced by how people tended to respond to them. He was praised, as his parents claimed, but in the form of supportive comments that implicitly encouraged the negative idea behind his statements. In effect, he got a pep talk for self-critical statements.

"You really did do a good job, Howie. I know you can do it all the time. You're just such a perfectionist. Don't worry so much."

Positive in themselves, his mother's words confirm pretty much what he thinks of himself: the idea of perfectionist and the suggestion that, while he should be able to do it right all the time, maybe he won't.

"Even when he feels he's done something that is out of the ordinary," his mother said, "he brushes aside any kind of praise. If we say, 'You did well,' he'll say, 'Big deal,' almost as if he's saying to himself, 'Sure, I did it, but the real me isn't that way.'"

Specific praise that is tied to behaviors that show him taking the initiative, being active even when there's a possibility of failure, is more likely to bypass Howie's feelings of worthlessness. It indicates both that he's done something out of the ordinary and that his parents care enough to pay close attention to what he did. At the same time, the praise ought not to refer to Howie's expressed feelings about himself, that he's not good enough, which would only reward his self-critical statements.

One small but telling incident illuminates how Howie's parents learned to use praise to define his worth, his grown-upness, and his ability to take an active part in the things going on around him. Howie, his mother and father, and his twelve-year-old sister went out to eat in a restaurant. In the past, when Howie had chosen something and it didn't turn out to be what he thought it should be, he'd say, "Oh, I never pick the right thing," or "I'm too dumb to pick something good, you do it." This day, when the waitress came to their table, he gave his order directly to her. It was a grown-up moment he clearly enjoyed, although he didn't draw any attention to what he had done by commenting on it afterward.

Later, however, his mother took him aside and talked about how he'd behaved. On other similar occasions she might have said, "See, you had no trouble picking something you like to eat tonight."

For a child with good feelings about himself it might be an adequate comment because he already knows how to do grown-up things like ordering food without worrying about doing it right. But for Howie, this kind of praise is too vague and also reminds him that he's done it in a way he thinks is "wrong" on other occasions.

More specific praise might be "I like the way you ordered in the restaurant. It was very grown-up." Still, it doesn't tell Howie anything out of the ordinary about his behavior.

What his mother said was a recreation of the scene in the restaurant that was as vivid as she could make it. "I like the way you ordered in the restaurant. You told the waitress in a very grown-up way that you wanted french fries instead of a baked potato. Then you told her what you wanted to drink and what kind of dressing on your salad. I was really proud of you tonight."

Faced with specifics and positive praise, Howie's "Yeah, but . . ." doesn't have a place to go. His parents have helped him take one small step toward a better self-image: I did something right, I behaved in a grown-up way, my mother liked the way I acted, I should like the way I act.

His parents carried over this kind of praise to everything they noted that showed taking-initiative behaviors, behaviors that shaped his world. And as they did it, Howie's fear of failure visibly diminished.

BEHAVIOR IN PARTS

Howie, like all children, will inevitably do something that's less than perfect. Parents have to sort out the nonvalued behaviors from the ones they wish to nurture. Bad doesn't cancel out good. Especially when you are trying to teach positive behaviors, you have to acknowledge both good and bad, being careful to not give too much attention to the negative but enough to the positive.

For example, Johnny has an accident playing ball. Five minutes later he comes into the house and tells his mother, "I was playing baseball and broke the window in the house across the street."

The behavior has two parts:

- Johnny has broken a window.
- He was honest; he told his mother what he'd done.

To encourage honesty and to keep the lines of communication open between parent and child, Johnny's mother may briefly reprimand him for breaking the window, to indicate this is not approved behavior. The temptation in a case like this is to make a dramatic scene, reminding Johnny that he's been told a hundred times not to play ball in that part of the yard, that he was careless, that he has no common sense. But this gives too much attention to the incident. His mother should spend much more time with him praising him for being honest about admitting what he'd done, and indicating that this is important to her, a sign of maturity: that honesty is a valued behavior.

Even if after having ordered well in the restaurant Howie spills his milk because he was behaving in a silly way, both parts of his behavior have to be viewed in perspective. Howie is still doing something right; something wrong doesn't cancel it out. He still should be praised.

THE POWER OF PRAISE

Praise is one of the most powerful teaching forces parents have at their command. It is a power that everyone can use to create warmth and caring between people. It works between friends, husbands and wives, employers and employees, and even strangers.

In the end, caring is the behavior most to be nurtured in our children. The resulting bonds of affection are the only certain source of what we want for them most, which is happiness.

The purpose of praise and its effects are threefold:

- Praise makes it likely that the praised behavior will occur more often in the future.
- Praise increases the child's self-esteem.
- Praise increases the bonds of affection between parent and child.

A few appropriate words of nurture, spoken at the right time, can have a strong immediate impact, but their greatest effect is in what happens later, long beyond childhood.

Chapter Eight

GAMES CHILDREN PLAY

The value of praise—the right kind of praise at the right time—can't be emphasized too much in raising children positively. Praise itself is a positive action, a giving rather than a taking away, encouragement rather than detraction.

Saying yes to your children is a far happier method of raising them than a constant no—all the negative aspects of criticism and sermons and energy wasted on what they've done wrong instead of what they do that's right and ought to be repeated. Yet as children acquire a growing repertoire of appropriate behaviors, they will test the limits of what they are allowed to do. If parents don't see this clearly, they can find themselves involved in games of behavior that carry a lot of emotional baggage and often burden them with a large dose of unnecessary guilt.

Parents need to avoid the games children play, even though their natural impulse may be to get caught up in the process and to justify themselves to their children as they would to another adult. Participating in such a game is tantamount to saying, "Go ahead and say I don't love you, or that you feel depressed, or that you're afraid of things, or that you're stupid, or that you tell lies because you're troubled about something, and I'll feel guilty enough to be a part of it by spending as much time as I can proving that what you're saying isn't so."

Spending time that way will practically guarantee that comments like "You don't love me" are going to be repeated in an ongoing game in which both players are losers.

Yet these kinds of behaviors and testing may have a certain validity in some situations: a child does need to know he's loved; sometimes a complaint is necessary. They need a positive response from a *parent*, not an argument from an adult who's been stung by the suggestion that he or she hasn't fulfilled his or her responsibilities.

"YOU DON'T LOVE ME"

Every parent has to deal at one time or another with that sure-fire attention-getter: "You don't love me"—or, equally effective, "You love Mary more than you love me."

The scenario goes something like this:

NINA: You don't love me.

PARENT (protesting, eager to reassure, even guilty): Of course I love you. I love you more than I can tell you. Why do you say that? Why do you feel this way?

Several responses like that, and the child will have learned which buttons to press to get a considerable reward in terms of time and attention, whether or not he actually feels "unloved." Yet the statement deserves an answer, without encouraging a repetition for the wrong (attention-getting) reasons.

Any parent is strongly tempted to respond with assurances, especially when the question of love is repeated: "Yes—yes, I love you; yes, you're important; yes, I care about you." But that's the wrong answer because it extends a false and unacceptable premise. What you have to say instead is something like: "Of course I love you, and you know it."

Even the child with good self-esteem is going to say, "You don't love me" once in a while. From time to time a child is going to see a situation where a brother or sister may appear to be favored—a privilege granted an older child, a surprise gift, anything that doesn't seem equitable. The problem is often expressed as "You don't love me," but the meaning is, "It's not fair."

The truth is, none of our lives are especially fair in terms of rewards. Blessings don't shower equally on everyone in the world outside the family or even within it. But encouraging the idea of "You don't love me" by allowing it to be discussed at length over and over again just to prove it isn't true, does a disservice both to the child and to the child's relationship with the parents. As Shakespeare pointed out, protesting too much suggests a possibility a charge is true; the question of whether things are fair suggests that nothing is fair and everything is open to complaint. I'll talk more about complaining later, in relation to larger problems in behavior, but the matter of love isn't something that needs to be repeatedly analyzed and defended.

A child who has a sense of self-esteem that makes him feel worthwhile isn't going to be troubled by day-to-day measurements of rewards and nonrewards as expressions of love. He's already feeling, "I'm okay, I'm competent, I'm as deserving of love as the next person." A moment of doubt is just that, not a way to command attention by saying the one thing that is sure to get total involvement from Mom or Dad.

Learn to say no to the testing, the demand for attention, while still saying yes to the fact of your love. No discussions or explanations, no rewards to prove that you do love your child. Just "You know that's not so. You know I love you." At some later time it's fine to give assurances of love for nothing at all, or for following a desired behavior—but not if there's a risk it will be associated in the child's mind with any earlier implicit demand.

Similarly, trying to find out *why* you have been accused of withholding your love plays along with the false premise and is equally unproductive. However long you talk, you won't uncover any deep reasons hidden away in the child's psyche. All you're ever likely to discover is that something happened that didn't fit in with your child's idea of the way things ought to be.

The way to show a child that you do love him or her is to take the time to say so when the child isn't asking for that reassurance. For example, try saying, "You know, Betty, I really love you" just because you feel like it, for no reason, or because she's done something that's lovable. If you feel guilty about possibly paying more attention to one child and less to another, again the time to make up for it isn't when the child confronts you with the charge, but later, in a situation unconnected with the challenge. You'll avoid the temptation to discuss the issue and you won't plant the idea that a guilt-provoking statement like "You don't love me" is going to be followed by total involvement on your part.

THE "FEELING SORRY" SYNDROME

Remember Annie Sullivan's comment to Helen Keller's mother about the potential destructive power of too much love and pity? Feeling sorry is an adult response, and while some parents feel a sort of formless guilt when a child starts to play the "You don't love me" game, others think the child has a reason for the accusation because of something they've done.

"With the divorce," one parent told me, "we've both been afraid to step too hard on Linda. We give her love to make up for the situation she's in, and we overlook a lot of things we normally wouldn't let her get away with. When you say this encourages manipulative behavior, you're right. I let her manipulate me, to make up for the divorce."

Linda's parents say they've heard of cases where divorced couples' kids wind up hating Mother or Father, and they're trying to avoid that. So they give in, both of them, to whatever Linda wants, because they feel guilty about breaking up the family. They want her to love them.

Feeling sorry and guilty is not a sound way to respond to a child's demands. The concern two adults may have about a divorce, for example, or being a working parent and not always available, shouldn't automatically grant a child the special right to play manipulative games.

Ed is described by his parents as "selfish, only caring about himself and his own feelings." He uses vile language to his parents and friends, and even hits his parents if he doesn't get his own way. His parents described him as a boy "with a lot of hang-ups," and they told me they felt sorry for him because he seemed to have "problems."

"I tell him that he is the most important person in the world," the mother said. "I feel so bad for him because he's got so many hang-ups, so I cater to him. 'Do you want me to get you a pillow? What would you like?' He's just a little kid, after all."

What Linda and Ed have both learned is that it pays to make their parents feel guilty. Their parents' reactions have taught them that when they repeatedly make demands, and especially if they suggest they feel unloved, they will get total time and attention. They are being rewarded for making their parents feel guilty.

In the short run, when the parents reassure them and give them what they ask because they feel sorry, there is brief peace. In the long run, feeling sorry and acting on it, giving the response that's demanded, only means the child will step up the demands. The cycle won't stop. And worse, the child will come to believe that the charges against his parents may be true.

Rewards for asking-for-love behaviors or making-Mother-and-Father-feel-guilty behaviors have another serious consequence: they will make the child unlovable to you and to others. It's a game with no winners at all. We can't give in to guilt; we have to encourage behaviors that don't play on our own hang-ups.

"NOBODY LIKES ME"

Some children learn to skate, to ride a bike, to cook. Others learn to complain. Complaining is a behavior a child learns like any other, even though it's not necessarily the kind that makes a big splash. Rather, it makes ripples that have a far-reaching effect. The child who's a complainer can turn off friends just as surely as by knocking them down or bossing them around. The complaining child ends up just as unhappy as the boy or girl who's not doing well in school, who doesn't get along with other children, or who wages a constant battle of defiance with parents.

Children are adept at the complaining game, although they may be somewhat less subtle than adults. The woman who complains about her husband, the man who complains about his boss, usually has a pretty good story to tell initially—until listeners grow weary of hearing the same litany of wrongs and turn away. Children complain in simpler terms:

"You don't love me; nobody loves me."

"Everybody picks on me."

"I'm stupid."

"My teacher doesn't like me."

"Nobody likes me."

Parents automatically respond to complaining statements like these with "Yes, I hear the unhappiness behind what you're saying, and I want you to tell me about it." It is as if a complaint signals a basic equation:

A child + a complaint = an unhappy child

and it touches off reassurance responses, understanding, caring, concern, the desire to take away the unhappiness and help the child have good feelings about him- or herself—if only we can find the problem that's causing the unhappiness, talk about it, solve it.

What might begin as a legitimate complaint (kids do pick on other kids, things do happen to make a child feel stupid, a hard-pressed teacher might seem to be unfair) often turns into an effective way of feeding the need for attention. The first couple of times deserve to be heard and discussed, but if that doesn't help the complaint, the tenth time won't either. Instead of solving a genuine complaint, parent and child are then giving the complaint problem status in itself, a tale to be told and retold, dissected and put together again. We're back to the myth of "Letting it all hang out," as if talking about problems and negative feelings will cause them to disappear.

Habitual whining and lamenting are just additional occasions to say no to your impulse to comfort and reassure, and to the child who complains for the attention it produces.

Talking about it won't give you a happy child.

Take, for example, the child who comes home and says to Dad, "I'm stupid."

"No you're not. You're a smart boy. Look at all the things you can do well, you can build model airplanes, you do well in school, you can play soccer. Why do you feel stupid? Did someone say that to you? Tell me what your problem is."

The recital of all the things he can do well that prove how smart he is sounds pretty good, and it represents a lot of positive attention from Dad. Let's try it again real soon.

It's much more valuable in terms of discouraging complaining behavior and encouraging a feeling of self-worth to say no: "No, you're not stupid."

Later, when the child has done something that's bright or clever, is the time to tell him he's smart.

"You glued the parts of that ship model very neatly, you're a smart boy. I'm proud of you."

The child has in his hands the well-made ship model, concrete proof that he's not stupid, reinforced with the praise and approval that build positive behavior.

"Everybody picks on me."

You can talk about it, with the best intentions in the world, knowing how bad it feels to be picked on or left out, or you can put the complaint in the proper perspective.

"What happened?"

"Well, the other kids wouldn't let me play with them today."

"That's not picking on you. Why didn't they let you play?"

"They already picked teams before I got there."

"That sounds fair enough. Maybe you can get there earlier tomorrow."

Children, like the rest of us, need sympathy and comfort for moments of unhappiness, but too much understanding, too much sympathy, too much effort to turn unhappiness to happiness, almost certainly will ensure that the complaint will be repeated.

Unfortunately, the child who learns to complain well, by getting a sympathetic response from parents, is going to turn off other people who don't care whether he's "happy" or not. People outside the family want to be with outgoing, caring people; they want to be with complainers as little as possible. And the loss of the satisfactions that others provide us, the lack of social relationships and caring, truly do make an unhappy person who now really has something to complain about.

It seems to me that the child who is taught to complain by well-meaning parents who, concerned about his or her well-being, are all too willing to say yes instead of no, is likely to become the adult who scans the world negatively, who is a pessimist, and who is "depressed" because of the limited satisfactions he or she finds in life.

How much easier for ourselves and our children if they never had the encouragement to find satisfaction in complaining and endlessly talking about negative feelings. And how ironic that parents' natural eagerness to have a happy child nurtures behavior that almost inevitably leads in just the opposite direction.

THE GAME OF SIBLING RIVALRY

Sibling rivalry is a game that may not exist, except in theories and the minds of parents and professionals who have been influenced by them.

Brothers and sisters don't always get along peacefully, and sometimes the conflict is profitable for the attention it creates. If there's a payoff for tormenting a sister or brother, it will continue, but not because of something inborn that makes brothers and sisters natural enemies. Some parents believe in the inevitability of sibling rivalry; they accept it and live with it, not understanding that their acceptance encourages the game to be played out to the unhappiness of all.

"Sibling rivalry" is a label that's been attached to a certain kind of behavior the professionals have found fascinating. Since their theories are based on negatives, they haven't come up with a term like "sibling caring." Language plays a big part in determining what we see; we have a label for conflict between brothers and sisters, so we see conflict more easily than we see caring, and with all good intentions tend to encourage what we see.

Sibling caring does exist. Brothers and sisters do care for each other; older siblings take care of younger ones; relationships among sisters and brothers are close and strong through long lifetimes. Younger siblings look up to their older brothers and sisters who, in turn, are protective of their younger siblings. Sibling caring is a real and positive bond, if parents take the time to see it and encourage it. The game of sibling rivalry occurs only if the referees—the parents—encourage it because they expect it to be there.

David likes to tease his younger sister. The more this behavior produces a response from her and from their parents, the more he does it. It's not long before they reach a point where his sister fights back and Mom and Dad step in. They've heard about sibling rivalry, and this must be it—a classic problem of parenting. The times David has helped his sister read a story, the day he taught her to ride a bike, the time he told her how pretty she looked, and the days he's waited to walk her home from school fade away and are forgotten.

Inadvertently, the observers of the game make it worthwhile by their concern.

Labels influence perception, what we see and what we don't see. People see sibling rivalry, but they don't take time to look for sibling caring. David's parents look for the problem whenever the two children are together. They step in quickly when he teases or annoys her.

"Leave your sister alone. Why do you bother her? Don't you like her? Are you jealous of her? Don't we treat you both the same way? Do you think we love her more?"

Spoken or unspoken, these questions color the relationship not only between the children but among all four family members. All this happens in the service of psychological theories that see only the negative and that break down the bonds of caring between brother and sister instead of building them up.

HOW TO CHANGE SIBLING RIVALRY TO SIBLING CARING

For years, psychologists have taught us that sibling rivalry is normal. Fortunately, this is a myth. Using some very simple methods, parents can change sibling rivalry to sibling caring—a term so positive that it is foreign to many psychologists.

One must begin this process at a time when there is no ongoing sibling rivalry. When the caring behavior occurs, jot it down on a small notepad; two or three examples a week are enough.

At a later time, thirty minutes to several hours afterward, at your convenience, follow the standard ABCD sequence:

A. Take your child aside, in private, and vividly remind him or her of the earlier sibling-caring behavior.

B. Immediately follow this with 100 percent praise, with no mention of less-caring behaviors of the past. Don't say, "It's nice to see you acting nicely toward your brother for a change."

C. Say why this caring behavior is valued. "It pleases me very much to see you reading to your sister and being so caring. This tells me you're really grown-up."

D. Immediately and casually follow this with five to fifteen minutes of pleasant time together. Don't say, "Because you were caring to your sister, I'll play a game with you." Just do it.

When you observe sibling rivalry, your response must be, above all, brief and dull. Don't try to find out how the fight began; no one ever begins fights. Investing your time and attention in an incident of sibling rivalry will only encourage more of the same behavior in the future.

THE "TO TELL THE TRUTH" GAME

Most games aren't played for fun but for the simple goal of getting attention. Some parental responses to games like dishonesty ("He's a born liar . . .") can have present and future consequences that can be very serious indeed. Children aren't born dishonest but learn that behavior, often as a way of getting attention.

Dennis, for example, had several brothers and sisters, none of whom were notably dishonest. Dennis, at ten, on the other hand, was a resourceful liar about almost everything. When his mother discussed his behavior and her concern, she couldn't understand why, among her seven children, one was a habitual liar.

"He won't tell the truth if his life depends on it. I'm so busy with all those kids, and everyone turned out well except Dennis."

When she talked more about her children, it was clear that she had only a limited amount of time to spend with each of them. Dennis wanted more time, and got it: by lying frequently and making her spend time trying to figure out whether he was telling the truth about everything. His mother had to make a special effort to keep track of whether he had actually given her back all the change from buying bread, or whether he had to stay after school, as he claimed, or had actually gone off with his friends without permission.

His "problem," unfortunately, is antithetical to an adult life where honesty is a valuable commodity, not only in dealings with the world in general but in adult personal relationships, where the sense of being able to trust another person is extremely important.

The attention-getting game of dishonesty is disturbing to parents, and in Dennis's case, the effort had to be made to see and encourage brief occurrences of truth-telling behaviors (not easy to uncover if parents have a firm belief that everything a child says is likely to be untrue). But for Dennis, there were times when he did give back the right change or when he did tell the truth, and was praised for it. And there were times when he fell into the game but no longer got a more than equal share of his mother's time; instead, the time she gave him followed only those behaviors she wanted to encourage.

DEBBIE'S NIGHTMARES
AND THE GAME OF FEAR

For weeks, five-year-old Debbie has been waking up screaming every night because of nightmares about "the big germ" and "the terrible lion."

Every night, her parents rush to her bedside to comfort and reassure her that there are no big germs, no lions, that her fears are groundless.

Before bed each night she asks, "Is everything safe?"

"You're safe," her mother tells her. "The shades are all pulled, the doors are locked, and we'll leave the night-light on."

The nightmares and fears still come, and during the day Debbie plays "the fear game," discussing her nightmares with her mother and anybody in the family who will listen. Her mother, for her part, sincerely believes that spending time

talking will help Debbie let out her feelings about the nightmares and will go a long way toward finding and removing
whatever problem is causing them.

By way of these long talks, Debbie's mother, without realiz-
ing it and with the best of intentions, is creating a problem
rather than solving one. She's telling Debbie that there is a very
real payoff for talking about fears, big germs, and terrible lions.
Not only is she being rewarded by becoming the center of attention day and night, but the more her parents talk about her
fears, the more they allow the fears to define her and the more
they communicate that there may be something to be afraid of.

In effect, Mother is saying, "I am worried about your fears; it
worries me so much that I will spend hours with you discussing
them. I am fearful, and the thing that makes me so are your big
germs and lions."

And Debbie's response is: "If Mother and Father are spending so much time talking about the terrible lion and the big
germ, that means they must be as worried as I am—so the lion
and germ must be real. If those grown-up people are worried,
then I, a little five-year-old, ought to be even more worried."

Because Debbie's parents have effectively said yes to her fears
and nightmares, they have found themselves caught up in a
perpetual cycle of nightmares and of talk about them that produces more talk, more nightmares, with a handsome reward
for Debbie in terms of attention—and frustration, worry, and
sleepless nights for her parents.

Behavior like Debbie's has to start somewhere. In her case,
we can trace it back to accidental happenings some months before. Debbie had the flu and a high fever. At the time, she talked
about bad dreams, and somebody else talked about germs. A
little while later, Debbie and her mother talked about a story
read at nursery school about "the terrible lion." An older brother
and sister teased her, telling her "the terrible lion will get you."

Then, one night, she had a real nightmare featuring big germs
and terrible lions, and Debbie found out that her parents' concern, warmth, and caring followed her being afraid of nightmares.

Obviously a child who has a nightmare should be comforted and reassured; there is no doubt that parents should be caring. We must, however, make a distinction between comforting a fearful child and going beyond comfort to searching for the root of the problem through long discussions. As soon as parents play psychoanalyst in their well-intentioned attempts to understand the problem, they may be setting up conditions for a negative relationship between themselves and the child that can be as interminable as analysis itself.

They may be creating a mountain from a molehill. In Debbie's case, her parents, instead of saying no and setting themselves limits in their concern about her fears, have taught her that nightmares and nightmare-related behaviors bring them closer, make them more involved with her. Those behaviors flourished, beyond Debbie's or her parents' control.

Is it possible to turn her behavior around, to stop the nightmares?

Yes, if Debbie can be provided with an alternative kind of behavior that also brings her parents close and demonstrates their involvement and caring. She needs to learn those behaviors that will promote emotional growth in place of nightmares, and ways to bring her parents close that encourage social development and ultimately feelings of self-worth. She has to learn the responsible, grown-up behaviors—opposite of being "afraid," of having nightmares—that will get her as much attention as waking up screaming every night.

LOOKING AT DEBBIE THROUGH NEW EYES

Debbie's parents have been saying yes to behaviors that are immature, dependent, and attention-getting, to the exclusion of most other kinds of activity. They have to learn to say no to the game and find new behaviors to say yes to. They have to learn to look at Debbie with new eyes.

The first step is to note specific examples of grown-upness, of mature, responsible, independent behavior consistent with Debbie's chronological age: getting her own cereal at breakfast time, answering the telephone in a grown-up manner, reading a book by herself, asking for something politely. These behaviors, whatever their motivation, are grown-up for a five-year-old, even though they are brief, ordinary, and commonplace. Once Debbie's parents have learned how to notice these small, quiet behaviors, they are in a position to use them to teach Debbie ways of bringing Mother and Father closer for positive, grown-up behavior rather than letting a five-year-old set the agenda with behavior that is fearful and immature. And together they will teach themselves new ways of dealing with the nightmares that neither encourage nor ignore them. In short, they learn how to teach their daughter by providing her with a somewhat changed world in which her feelings of self-worth and positive behavior are most important.

Here's a list of Debbie's grown-up, responsible behaviors that her parents made note of in one week:

- She went upstairs alone to change her dress.
- She said "Thank you" when her grandmother gave her a gift.
- She helped her mother carry plates and silverware out to the backyard picnic table.
- She answered the telephone and took a message from a neighbor for her mother.

Each time Debbie behaved in a positive, grown-up way, her mother or father told her specifically what about her behavior pleased them: what she did, what she said, how she said it that was grown-up—not simply a general comment about acting grown-up.

"It was very grown-up of you to change your clothes by yourself. That pleased me a lot."

"You said thank you so politely to Grandma when she gave you the present. I was proud of you for being so grown-up."

"I like it when you help me set the picnic table like a grown-up."

"You took the message from Mrs. Jones very well, that was very grown-up of you."

The seeds of positive behavior have been planted.

An hour or two later, Mother takes Debbie aside and as vividly as possible reconstructs for her what she did earlier, the grown-up behavior that was so pleasing.

"You carried all the knives and forks out to the picnic table, like a grown-up person, and it was so helpful to have you set the table with me. You do it very well, and I'm so pleased."

Immediately and casually, Mother follows her praise with five or ten minutes doing something that Debbie enjoys—reading a story, singing a song together, just having Debbie sit on her lap and talk. Mother is careful not to say, "Because you were grown-up, I'll read you a story." This avoids future bargaining: "Because I did this, you owe me a story."

It can be amazing how quickly specific praise encourages behavior that is grown-up and responsible, as in Debbie's case. The time and attention she gets in this slightly changed world, where she is viewed with new eyes, are as valid to her as the attention induced by nightmares—and far more satisfying.

Debbie has been given a reason to behave in a positive way . . . but what about the nightmares? It's time now to make an effort to minimize the attention given them.

When Debbie wakes up now, or talks about her fears, her mother listens, expresses a few words of comfort, and that's all. There are no more long discussions about them, no reminders that she has fears ("Did you have a bad dream last night?"), no opportunities to communicate Mother's worries to Debbie. If Debbie's getting the kind of parental involvement she wants from positive behavior and minimal involvement for negative behavior, she's going to reduce her investment in the "big germ" and the "terrible lion," and they aren't going to live in her mind the way they have in the past.

Debbie's story is just one of hundreds of cases where parents have learned how to teach their children positive behavior in the place of negative attention-getting. Instead of playing along in childhood games—in the testing of how far a child can go to get noticed—the parents have substituted a system of positive nurturing through praise and shared time. That system can be applied to a wide range of behavioral problems that develop, usually inadvertently, when parents allow the negatives to take charge of behavior.

It isn't difficult to see the positive if you look for it, and it's easy to use the positive to teach your child behaviors that bring happiness.

Chapter Nine

YOU DON'T HAVE TO MOVE TO CHANGE YOUR CHILD'S ENVIRONMENT

At seven-thirty on a weekday morning, Mrs. Brown is in the kitchen preparing breakfast for seven-year-old Gregory and his ten-year-old sister, Pat. They haven't appeared yet, so she's enjoying a cup of coffee and giving thanks that, so far, the day has been peaceful. She doesn't have to leave for her part-time job for several hours. As is often the case, her husband is out of town on business.

"Hurry up, you two," she calls upstairs. "You'll be late for school."

Pat joins her almost immediately, but there's no sign of Gregory.

"Where's your brother?"

"Oh, he's fooling around with some stuff in his room," Pat says.

"Get moving, Greg," his mother calls. "And don't forget to make your bed." She assumes that, as usual, he'll refuse.

When Gregory finally makes his appearance, he doesn't disappoint her. "I don't feel like it," he says by way of greeting. "You can't make me."

"Don't start," his mother says. "What's bothering you today? You know you're supposed to make the bed."

"I won't. Is that the only jelly doughnut?"

"Yes. You and Pat can split it."

"I don't want to split it, I want the whole thing."

"Gregory," his mother says, "you can't always have it your way. You have to learn to share."

"I don't care," says a furious Gregory. "I want it." He tells her at length why he should get it all.

Mrs. Brown feels her own anger rising. "Look, I don't know what's eating you this morning, but if I hear one more argument from you—"

Gregory doesn't wait. He's out the door, knocking over a chair on his way, with a parting yell, "I hate you!"

Pat grabs her books and goes off to school, leaving Mrs. Brown alone to contemplate the scene that has just passed.

TAKING STOCK

Gregory doesn't like her, he won't do anything she asks, he has no idea what it is to be unselfish, his anger at the most trivial things upsets her. At least today they didn't get into the long discussions they usually have. Mrs. Brown tries so hard to understand her son, to figure out what is bothering him that he should always behave this way. She feels it must be that because she went back to work when he started school a couple of years before, he hasn't gotten the same attention Pat got when she was smaller. She should be able to get to the root of his problem, but it's hopeless. She doesn't understand what's going on in his head, but she's pretty sure she's to blame: Gregory doesn't have any problems at school. His teachers have always found him cooperative and not at all difficult. He seems to take as much pleasure in pleasing them as he does in fighting her.

"I'm convinced he's going to end up as a juvenile delinquent," she says. "His temper is terrible, and I know he thinks I don't care about him. That hurts me so much. I just don't know what I've done to make him this way. Something's bothering him, and somehow it's my fault."

Faced with the frustrations of dealing with behavioral problems such as Gregory's, most of the time a parent will say, "I blame myself, it must be something I did to give him a problem. I see what's going on, but I don't understand why. If I understood him, I could help him, but I don't, so I can't do anything."

There's one response I have to parents who decide they're to blame for their children's bad behavior, who throw up their hands in despair over their guilt and failure to understand what's happening. I tell them, "If you plan every morning all the things you're going to do to make your child unhappy, make him behave badly, make him lose his friends or do poorly in school, cause him to be defiant, then go ahead and feel guilty—you've earned the right. But if you've done what you think is best for your child, and it hasn't worked, there is no reason to feel guilty— and your sense of guilt becomes a part of the problem. Rather, we should look at some better ways of relating to your child."

"We don't try to make our child unhappy," every parent will protest. "Still . . . *something* is causing a problem."

We are back to trying to root out the demon, the thing that's troubling the child and shows up as surface behavior. A crucial point here is parents' confused idea of what their reality is. All too many believe that the reality of the situation is the psychological reason behind the behavior. As we have seen, it is all but impossible to uncover any psychological reasons for behavior; it's impossible to understand in those terms.

GETTING IN TOUCH WITH REALITY . . .

Instead, for our reality we have to look to the environment in which the behavior takes place, the things that encourage it, good or bad. It's time for parents to take a good long look at what the environment feels like. Is it full of anger and frustrations and sermons about behavior? Or is it one where positive and valued behaviors are recognized and praised?

If you're willing to stop taking all the responsibility for your child's behavior, if you want to understand it in ways that offer real insight and lead to improvements, stop looking for hidden meanings and try to see what's going on right before your eyes. Certainly that should include an examination of the part you have played in creating an environment that gives negative behavior the room and nurture to flourish. If you still feel you have to take some of the blame, fine—but then make the effort to break this guilt-driven cycle of cause and effect, behavior and consequences. Step back and take an objective view of your child's behavior and the environment in which it takes place.

You can correct what's not right by changing the environment and the way that behavior is rewarded. This may lack the glamour and depth of the psychological approaches to behavior, but those lead nowhere. We have to face reality, then reconstruct the environment to give it a new, positive feeling.

But at the outset, Gregory's mother still worries about the reality beneath the surface. She wants to understand.

"He doesn't trust me," she says. "He'll believe anybody—his friends, his grandfather, his sister, his father—before he'll believe what I tell him. It's usually a silly thing, like whether Superman is a real person. I'll say no, it's just a story, and he'll tell me he doesn't believe me, because one of the kids says Superman is real. I want him to think he can trust what I say."

And how does she react when he seems not to "trust" her? When he begins the day with a refusal to make his bed, demands for the whole doughnut, and a furious exit?

"I get angry," she admits. "I've tried talking to him calmly, but he's so stubborn that I get madder and madder and then I end up wanting to strangle him. I just can't talk to him. I *can't find out what's bothering Gregory. He won't share it with me.*"

What does she see?

"I see a very troubled little boy, who no longer knows how to control his temper, who has a lot of resentment against his mother, and who hasn't developed a sense of caring and sharing. I see a problem there that has to be solved if he'd just open up to me."

The pervasive belief that somehow you have to understand what's bothering a child in order to make sense of his behavior clearly affects the way Gregory's mother looks at him. If only she knew what the problem in Gregory's head is, she'd be able to help him get rid of it. Or would she? Parents in that situation seldom go beyond trying to understand the so-called problem to figuring out exactly what is happening, why it is happening, and how it can be stopped.

. . . AND TURNING IT AROUND

The way Mrs. Brown should be seeing Gregory and his behavior is in terms of the environment in which it takes place: not the tables and chairs and his breakfast and the disputed doughnut, but what is actually going on. Then she can change her own part in it.

At seven-thirty she's in the kitchen getting breakfast ready for Gregory and Pat.

Gregory refuses to make his bed, as he always does. This time, though, his mother doesn't argue. There's nothing bothering Greg, except perhaps a dislike of making beds.

"Is that the only jelly doughnut?"

"Yes. You and Pat can split it."

"I want the whole thing."

"Split it or Pat gets it all. Or maybe I'll eat it."

Sure, Greg wants the whole doughnut—and he wouldn't mind getting all the available attention along the way. But that's the extent of the problem. He doesn't feel his sister gets more attention than he does, or that his mother doesn't care about him. He isn't warped from birth or suffering from a mental illness. However, he's willing to push for both the doughnut and the attention right up to whatever limits are set for him.

"Gregory, I don't want to discuss it anymore. Don't be late for school."

He's out the door, knocking over a chair on his way. "I hate you!"

"I'm sorry you do," his mother says. She's done nothing to make him hate her, she is a caring mother. Gregory is still trying to get her attention, this time with behavior he hopes will force a confrontation about his abusive words. Because it doesn't work, he's less likely to try it again.

This is one way of looking at the reality of behavior rather than trying to find out what's "bothering" him. If anyone asked him to analyze why he really acts the way he does, little Greg wouldn't have a clue—a situation that in other circumstances might provide a therapist with many profitable years in pursuit of the phantom problem. But the only problems worth looking at are his behavior and what to do about it. Greg already knows if he screams long enough, raises enough confusion, causes his mother enough anguish and anger, she rewards him with attention. So one solution is to eliminate that payoff.

Greg's environment consists of responses, usually negative ones for negative behavior, as in the earlier kitchen scene. He's learned how to behave in that kind of environment. It has nothing to do with what his mother does or doesn't understand.

If the environment provides equally strong rewards for good behaviors in the same class (say, grown-upness) as for the kinds that cause trouble, isn't it logical that the bad behavior will change as rewards for negative behavior are withdrawn? And isn't an atmosphere of trust and closeness and caring preferable to one that just plain feels bad, full of anger and disputes and slammed doors?

Yes on both counts. But how do you reshape the environment? By eliminating the hostility and defiance and replacing them with conditions that encourage positive behavior. But don't expect that a few seconds of praise will change things overnight. You can't immediately undo the patterns that have been created by hours of attention given for negative behaviors.

Gregory's situation is a good example of how a loving mother, one who cares about her child and wants him to care for her, sets up the conditions for negative behavior. In an effort to understand, she pays a good deal of attention to the behavior. In a perfectly normal way, she gets angry when her seven-year-old defies her. With good justification, she's upset when he cries and kicks the furniture. Like any mother, she wants him to have what she thinks will make him happy, whether it's the last doughnut or watching a television show. Like every parent, she wants her son to trust her, and she sees a refusal to believe her as indicating lack of trust. Yet those disputes about Superman have nothing to do with trust and a lot to do with the time Mother spent trying to convince Gregory she was right.

All of these things taken together mean that Gregory is the center of attention in the home environment; the more disruptive he is, the more attention he gets. He's learned to behave in ways that are sure to get total involvement from his mother.

The first step in changing the feel of the environment is for Gregory's mother to put aside her guilt about being the cause of what's bothering him. She didn't do anything intentionally to create his behavioral problems, and feeling guilty solves nothing.

The next step is for her to try seeing him with new eyes, to look at his behavior objectively, and instead of saying that he's defiant, untrusting, and uncaring, learn to see exactly what it is he does that is, for example, stubborn—what specific kind of behavior ought to be changed. Those new eyes must also learn to see fleeting moments of good behavior. Not simply that "sometimes he's good," but that sometimes "he picks up his clothes when I ask him to"; sometimes "he lets his sister choose the TV program we'll watch"; sometimes "he goes to bed on time without a scene."

The new eyes will recognize these actions as examples of sibling caring, Mother Theresa behavior, and so forth; indicators that he is thinking of the needs, feelings, and wishes of others.

He needs to be (A) reminded of the behavior at a later time; (B) given 100 percent praise with no conditions or holding back; (C) told that the behavior means it's grown-up to think of other people; and (D) given special time doing something enjoyable with one or both parents immediately after those three steps.

The examples of what Gregory does without making waves in the household—brief, expected, apparently insignificant moments in themselves—are the new standards for beginning to reshape their shared environment. It doesn't matter, either, what the motivation for these small moments was, that he went to bed without an argument simply because he was tired, or that he didn't want to watch television anyhow, or that for some reason he didn't think twice about picking up his clothes. What matters is that they happened. They are moments of quiet, valued behavior, and they need nurture through the ABCD sequence.

The encouragement for these behaviors comes in the form of a reward, just as bad behavior was rewarded with a powerful response of anger and argument. The reward for positive, non-defiant behavior is praise, along with time and attention. As soon as that starts happening, a little bit of the environment changes; Greg is getting what he wants without paying the price of being a monster, and he experiences moments of feeling good and worthwhile—the teachable moments when he is listening, hearing what his mother has to say about what pleases her, about what she considers valued behavior.

It appears that the moments of defiance, in Greg's view at least, are a sign that he's independent and growing up, although in a negative rather than positive way. "You can't make me" translates into "I'm a big boy, I don't have to listen to you." How can his mother encourage him to be truly independent without at the same time nurturing the shouting; to be grown-up without the tears; to be responsible without the slammed doors?

The answer is that she has to take note of all those times, however brief, when he does do things that really are grown-up and responsible, and then must praise them, make them worthwhile, give him a reason for repeating them rather than the disruptive behaviors that so distress her.

It's easy to make a list of the ordinary, quiet moments and specific, concrete actions that reflect the kind of behavior parents want to see all the time: behavior that expresses the abstract values this household, these parents, think are important for their children.

So Gregory helped carry the bags of groceries into the house. Why not? He eats here, too. But it's thoughtful and caring, and it doesn't matter that the real reason he helped is that he wanted to know whether Mom bought the kind of ice cream he said he liked; his motivation isn't relevant. The point is that it's worthwhile behavior, and his mother makes a note of it.

And later, an hour, two, or more, Gregory's mother takes him aside, in private, while his sister is watching television or doing her homework, and says, "You helped me carry in all those bags of groceries today. That was very thoughtful and grown-up, and it pleased me a lot. I like to see you acting grown-up."

Gregory's mother is labeling his behavior as valuable; she likes seeing him act in a grown-up way. Mother Theresa behavior shows he is thinking of other people's needs, feelings, and wishes; behaviors centered on other people are real signs of maturity, and she's praising him. And Gregory, for that moment, isn't going to respond with "No," or a fit of crying. He's going to listen to those words that build up the image of himself as a big boy. His mother knows enough to not say something like, "It's nice to see you helpful for a change." Gregory doesn't need reminders of his frequent difficult behavior.

Quickly and casually at the same time as the praise, Gregory's mother suggests that they do something together that she knows he will enjoy. Perhaps they spend five or ten minutes talking about his science project or the fortunes of his favorite major-league baseball team. Maybe they play a game or look through a catalog of sporting equipment. Enjoyable time with Mother, as compared with those less enjoyable moments when there's defiance on one side and anger on the other and no communication of values at all, creates a totally different atmosphere. The environment has a new feel to it, and it's surprising how quickly children recognize and respond to the change.

Gregory's mother is careful not to say or imply, "Because you were so grown-up, I'll play a game with you." You don't make contracts for good behavior. The reality has to be more subtle; the connection has to be between the action and the praise. The "reward," which is the game and the time spent together, reinforces the praise; it doesn't replace it.

If Gregory does voice the idea, "You're playing this game with me because I carried in the groceries," his mother doesn't acknowledge it. She might simply say, "You know, it makes me feel good when you help me."

The element of praise has been added to a household that had seen little of it, not because Gregory's mother didn't care or didn't want to praise him, but because the old environment was one in which the tone was set by the conflict between mother and son. It needed some extra effort on the mother's part to see the small moments of quiet, positive behavior that were all too often overshadowed by the battles between them.

IN THE FACE OF DEFIANCE

Gregory's defiant behaviors are his way of getting attention, proving that he is a big boy and his own person, who can't be told what to do. The only way to change those behaviors is to help make him feel an inner sense of worth as a more mature young man. The more positive he feels about himself, the fewer reasons he will have to be defiant.

Start by keeping a diary, without telling him. List four to six specific examples of the following types of mature behaviors weekly: sibling caring; taking disappointment calmly; Mother Theresa behaviors (see Chapter 6 for descriptions and examples). Note such behaviors even if they're brief, even if ordinary, even if expected, even if Gregory does them all the time. Then follow the ABCD sequence between thirty minutes and seven to eight hours after each specific behavior (see "Communicating Values" in Chapter 5).

PROSPECTING FOR POSITIVES

There are always three to five incidents in the course of a week that reflect the behavior that ought to be encouraged. The investment in time for praise and a few minutes of enjoyable activity together is quite small. The consequences can be highly gratifying for both parent and child. The child seeks more of those moments that feel good and build self-esteem; the parent is helping to build a new emotional environment that brings the child closer and makes for increased feelings of warmth and affection between parent and child.

It should be emphasized that this method of praise and reward is not a manipulative approach to bringing about changes in behavior. A major difference from the old approach is that it is conscious, of course, whereas the conditions bringing about the negative behavior were largely unintentional. Gregory's mother wasn't aware of the relationship between his attention-getting tantrums and the time and response she gave them; she was wrapped up in concern about her guilt, his lack of caring, his feeling that she didn't care about him, and on and on. Operating on the basis of insights to behavior and consequences is a far better approach to the relationship than working in the dark. She is modifying her own behavior as a way of improving Gregory's, with a view to changing their common environment. Whether they act consciously or on impulse, all parents have a tremendous influence on their children. In this case the original result was the accidental nurturing of behavior that was negative. When she realized her error, Gregory's mother shifted her rewards of time and attention to behavior she considered valuable.

All this method does is remind parents of children with behavioral difficulties how to take a step-by-step approach to encouraging positive behavior. It's a conscious effort on the parents' part, but just as the child soon learns that he doesn't need constant verbal praise, because he knows his parents are aware of what he's doing, so the parents establish a habit of praise and encouragement that becomes almost automatic— no lists, no planned enjoyable time, just spontaneous responses to what the child does that pleases them.

MEANWHILE . . .

Even though Gregory's mother began encouraging grown-up behavior and channeling the defiance and the desire to be an independent person into positive areas, she also still had to deal with his tears, the slammed doors, and the arguments when he didn't get his way; the old patterns don't just melt magically away in a couple of weeks. She couldn't continue to let him have his own way, but now she was able to deal with such moments far more intelligently, minimizing the attention she gave for negative behavior.

Back before she knew how to deal with it, Greg's mother had always been aware that she often gave in to him too readily just to keep him quiet. She had tried not to give in every time, because she knew it encouraged him in the notion that if he kept at her long enough he'd end up getting his way. But even when Greg didn't prevail, he still had the option of screaming and crying and getting attention when his mother tried to find out what was bothering him. Since she agreed to assume that nothing was bothering him, and that a firm refusal to give in to his demands wasn't going to make his hypothetical problem any worse and might serve to help change his difficult behavior, the effort to say no came easier.

"No, you can't have it your way this time, and we're not going to discuss it any further."

Initially, almost any child with Greg's history is going to re-double his efforts to get his way, and for a time the crying and anger will actually increase. After all, this kind of behavior has always worked before; now that it's met resistance, let's just push it up a notch or two in the hope of getting the old response. If nothing happens, and at the same time there's a constant stream of praise for what he does that pleases his mother, the negative behavior becomes less and less worthwhile.

Of course, it's difficult for a caring parent to see her child apparently wanting something so much that he reacts in a way we interpret as unhappy. And of course it's natural for a parent to be angry or annoyed in a head-to-head confrontation with a child who's determined to have his way. Again, the only re-sponse that works is to refuse to be drawn into a discussion or an argument, and to make that refusal as firm and as brief as possible.

A very real reason why the method of changing a child's behavior described here has proven so effective for preteen-age children is that the environment we are dealing with is a limited one and the primary sources of praise and encourage-ment are the home and the parents. Once a child moves into adolescence and adulthood, the environment broadens to in-clude the outside world complete with pressure from peers and other adults in various roles. But outside influences on pre-teens are usually just the child's classmates and teachers. At that critical time of life, parents have more influence over the quality of the child's environment—and more opportunity to influence it for the child's good—than they or anyone else will ever have again.

Chapter Ten

CHILDREN WITHOUT FRIENDS: NURTURING EMOTIONAL INTELLIGENCE

Nothing is more worrisome to parents than a child's lack of friends. Why does one child have a knack for popularity with friends and classmates while another has an equal aptitude for driving kids away? Why do some invariably react to other children in ways that are guaranteed to create hostility: being bossy and demanding, starting fights, being selfish—the children Goleman describes as "out of synch," who relate to others in ways that lead to discomfort rather than friendship, who are inarticulate in the unspoken language of feelings. Why do some children seem to withdraw into quiet corners and refuse to make any effort at all to involve themselves with others?

"Don't all children want friends?" a parent asked me. "Doesn't Billy see that everything he does guarantees that they're never going to come near our house again if they can help it?"

Learning to make friends, even at a very young age, is a behavior like any other. It's taught by having the seeds of making-friends behaviors cultivated, and it flourishes as the satisfactions of having friends provide their own rewards. Unfortunately, losing-friends behaviors can also develop if the wrong behavior is encouraged, even in the most inadvertent ways.

Parents can be slow to see the problem developing; it's easier to blame the other children, to attribute a lack of friends to shyness, to write off incidents with "Children will be children." When it becomes obvious the child simply doesn't have any friends, the first thought parents have is to find some.

"We sent him to camp for a month so he'd make some new friends," a mother said about a boy nobody liked to be with. "He hated it, because nobody wanted to be his friend even there."

Putting a child who drives away friends in touch with other children is not going to bring friends; it will only bring more enemies. A child has to be taught how to be a friend.

"HER OWN WORST ENEMY"

The parents of ten-year-old Maria said, "She's had more than her share of unhappiness because she's her own worst enemy when it comes to other children.

"We worry a lot about the things she's always doing that are making her lonely and friendless. She doesn't play well, wants to have it her way. Sometimes she's just plain unpleasant, and it's gotten so that nobody will come over here to play; they certainly don't call her up to play with them.

"We began to think that Maria had some deep psychological problem, because both of us have a lot of friends. We like being with people, and I think they like to be with us. I know Maria is only ten, but I have a picture of her going through life being left out of everything that life has to offer—you know, the girl who is left at home on prom night because nobody wants to ask her out. And then we got to thinking about what we read, the children who get involved as teenagers with drugs and stuff like that because it's the only way they have of connecting with other people. Children like that are losers, and it's upsetting to think of your ten-year-old as a loser already. We don't know what we did to make it happen.

"It crossed our minds that if only she *acted* differently, she wouldn't have this problem about friends, but what more could we do? We thought we'd raised her properly, and we were completely at a loss about what to do, except take her to a therapist who could find out what was troubling her.

"The therapist told us it might take years to unravel Maria's problems. Well, as far as we were concerned, she didn't have years. We wanted to do something that would work right now, help her to have friends before it was too late."

The method I've described helped Maria build up her winning-friends behavior with praise and encouragement from her parents. It did help her to act differently, just as her parents wanted, and it did, slowly but surely, bring children her own age to her.

"I made a list," her mother said, "noting the times when she did things that reached out to others in a positive way, and I'm ashamed that I had put so little effort before into seeing the good things about Maria. She's wonderful with her little sister, for example, who's four years younger. Except when she's being stubborn and willful, she *always* says 'Please' and 'Thank you.' I guess it was such expected behavior we never paid much attention. There were other things, too, that we'd never learned to see and encourage. The little boy next door had a broken leg, and Maria was out there the first day he was up, helping him walk on his crutches. I think she was just fascinated by the idea of crutches, but she was pleased when we took her aside later and told her that helping someone like that was what people liked in a friend. And she was out there the next day with him, helping out again.

"Soon after, my sister from out of state came to stay for a couple of days, and brought with her Maria's cousin, who's only a year younger. The two girls seemed to get along well—Maria classified her more as a guest than a playmate at first and behaved well. That gave us a good opportunity to take her aside and express our pleasure at specific things she did with her cousin, and make the connection between that and what people like to see in a friend.

"We kept at it, praise and encouragement and time together with Maria that she enjoyed, and in an amazingly short time we saw a real change in her. Because she'd offended so many of the children at school and in the neighborhood, she didn't have a whole lot of friends all at once. But gradually one or two started coming around regularly. What a relief for us and for Maria."

MORE ENCOURAGEMENT
THROUGH PROMPTING

Maria's parents also helped her strengthen some of the social skills she needed to make and keep friends. They gave her additional supports for her positive behavior through gentle pushes or prompts that helped encourage existing making-friends behavior and gave her additional new skills of the same kind.

Prompts can be useful, but they have to be brief and relatively infrequent so that they don't end up as parental nagging. Once or twice a week, her mother would casually suggest that Maria make some effort to bring friends to her: "Why don't you call up Nancy and have her come over to play Monopoly?" Or "How would you like to have Tina come over to lunch today?"

If Maria failed to take up the suggestion, no more was said about it. If she did respond to the prompt and called the other child, her mother was able to take Maria aside later and remind her of what she had done.

Reminder: "It was nice of you to have Nancy over to play Monopoly."

Praise: "You took turns very well. I like to see you doing things like that, like a good friend."

Enjoyable time: "Let's get out our bikes and take a ride around the neighborhood."

Prompting, if it's gentle, brief, appropriate, and infrequent, can be an effective way of bringing children together so that those who are like Maria will have a chance to use and expand their making-friends behavior. Parents are able to see the opportunities and encourage the child to take the initiative with other children.

NOTICING THE QUIET BEHAVIORS

When I first met Judy's parents, her mother said of her relationships with other children, "She gets along all right, but without any real friends."

In order to put Judy in better touch with her classmates both in and out of school, I proposed encouraging those behaviors that will make them want to be with her and seek her out as a friend. Some of the specific behaviors to be rewarded and nurtured, which I listed with the help of her parents, were sharing pens and pencils, taking turns during a game, laughing appreciatively at a classmate's joke, telling a girl she liked her sweater, thanking a classmate, asking other students about their vacation plans, giving an appropriate gift, helping a classmate with a math problem, and holding animated conversations. I emphasized the importance of being specific, of describing exactly what Judy said and did when they praised her for one of these behaviors.

They agreed to note two to three examples each week with the usual caveats—*even if they are brief, even if they are ordinary, even if they are expected behaviors, even if she does them all the time, no matter what the motivation, and no matter what happened before or afterward.*

I reminded them to look for ordinary, not necessarily extraordinary, examples of these behaviors. On those occasions when such behaviors were observed, the parents were to note specifically what she said and did, and one to six hours later, at their convenience, were to take her aside and attempt to make that earlier situation come to life again by describing it vividly. They then quickly told her what the behavior meant to them—for example, "It's the kind of thing people like in a friend"—and they immediately praised her. "This was really wonderful behavior and it makes us terribly proud you're so good about the needs of others."

A couple of times a week, this would be *immediately* and *casually* followed by spending five to ten minutes with her, talking about something she enjoys or engaging in an activity the parents know she likes. It was done as though the idea had just occurred to them at that moment, not "because you have done such and such, I will allow you to do this or that."

Telling Judy she played well or seemed to get along with Johnny when they were playing that morning is unlikely to encourage the good peer-relationship behaviors. It doesn't tell her what she needs to know about the specific behaviors, such as sharing some object or listening to what the other child has to say, that go into making good relationships.

Again, the teachable moment occurs immediately following words of praise. If the parents want to communicate values and ideals that are important to them, it is best to do it immediately following praise for behaviors that represent even small examples of those values such as honesty or successfully relating to kids her own age—"That's the kind of thing people like in a friend."

FRIENDS AND SCHOOL

The one setting in which children are most in touch with other children is, of course, at school. On the playground and in the classroom they're interacting with each other for many hours a day, five days a week, and it's here that friends are made or opportunities for friendship missed. Very often teachers see most clearly that a boy or girl is having trouble making or keeping friends. They see the child left alone at recess or being the last one chosen for a team. They see the classroom behavior that indicates other children don't want to associate with the child. Teacher and parents can sometimes work together to help a child learn making-friends behaviors and to discourage the behaviors that drive other children away.

Eight-year-old Paul, on many occasions, demonstrates his desire to reach out to other children. Sometimes it's positive and sometimes it's not, and Paul is left in a kind of limbo in relation to other children.

"He often tries to please his classmates," his teacher says, "but sometimes to the point of going overboard about it. He anticipates other students' needs, offers them pencils and rulers and the like, before they even want them. He's good at math, so he's always offering to help explain math problems."

Yet Paul is a loner; the others don't seek him out.

His teacher: "I've seen him wandering aimlessly around the playground like a lost soul."

His parents: "He just doesn't seem to have many friends; he's a loner."

"That's what's so hard for Paul, I think," his teacher says. "He makes a real effort to reach out to the other children by offering them assistance and his possessions, and for a minute, maybe, there's some kind of bond between them. Then Paul invariably turns around and blows it. He'll do something that almost guarantees nobody will be friends with him."

He does things, it turns out, that make people notice him. He's a tattletale, according to his teacher, and she remembers several occasions when he's sparked some kind of conflict, calling one boy a show-off because he was walking through the lunchroom with a girl, calling another a dummy because he'd made a mistake in class.

The child who is tattled on by Paul, or the boys who are called names by him, are definitely brought closer to him. They won't ignore him. Similarly, the boy or girl who Paul helps out with math or who borrows his ruler also isn't ignoring him.

Paul needs to learn new ways of reaching out to children to bring them closer to him, not because they are angry or because of his occasional potentially worthwhile gestures of generosity, but in ways that are enduring and constant.

The primary goal is to help teach children like Paul those behaviors that make other children want them as a friend: to teach them to break the ice in an appropriate way—to reach out and then to learn behaviors that maintain the relationships. In Paul's case, his teacher, along with his parents, made the effort, following the method already outlined.

The teacher observed examples of appropriate behavior to be used as the basis for praise and encouragement—however brief, expected, ordinary, whatever the motivation, and no matter what happened before or after. An incident of name-calling, for example, doesn't cancel out an appropriate making-friends behavior before or after it. There were already the occasions when Paul helped with math or shared a pencil; the teacher learned to see others.

"I didn't hear the joke, but Paul responded to something one of the other boys said with a comment that made everyone laugh, really laugh."

In the later moment when the teacher took Paul aside, he was praised for having a good sense of humor, and reminded that people like to have friends who can make them laugh.

During art activity period, Paul offered a couple of his colored marking pens to a new boy who had just come into the class. When the teacher praised Paul for being generous, it was also made clear that his behavior toward a new student helped to make the boy feel comfortable, and that's a good, making-friends way to act.

The rewards following praise and the communication of values during the teachable moment are, in school, things like carrying a message to the school office, being in charge that day of the classroom plants or animals, being allowed independent activity, or, if the teacher has time, talking for several minutes about something that interests Paul.

At home, Paul's parents, too, followed the method for encouraging making-friends behaviors, and they used prompting as Paul began to respond to praise and reach out in more positive ways to friends. The new boy in school was invited over to play, at Paul's mother's suggestion, and the two boys played happily. Later, she reminded Paul specifically of what they did and how much it pleased her. The praise and the few minutes she and Paul spent together doing something he liked helped build Paul's image of himself as a good friend and made it worthwhile for him to continue to behave in ways that encourage friendships.

"HE'S JUST SILLY"

Norman, on the other hand, could be seen by his teacher as really discouraging friendships. His parents labeled him as "shy." Shy behavior, however, is usually interpreted by other children as rejection; and they don't want to be with someone who rejects them.

How did Norman specifically discourage friendships? His teacher was able to make a list of examples.

He kept to himself. For instance, when he came into the classroom, he tended not to talk to the other students, kept his head down, and was very quiet and nonassertive.

He rejected overtures of friendship. When Betty offered him her eraser, he said in a very gruff and rejecting way, "I don't need that." When a boy asked Norman if he liked the cartoon he'd drawn, Norman didn't respond at all, as if he simply didn't know what to say in such a situation.

He was sometimes demanding. When his paper blew off his desk, instead of getting it himself, he said, "Get that for me."

For Norman, because he seemed not to know what to say or do in situations that might ordinarily lead to friendship, his teacher and his parents at home used gentle prompting to encourage social skills that help make friends.

For example, the teacher made a special effort to say, "Good morning, Norman," when he came into the classroom. It's not likely that a child like Norman (or any child) is always going to imitate the teacher's friendliness, but she can push just a little and say, "Tomorrow when you come into class, when someone says hello, why don't you say hello or good morning back?"

When Betty offers her eraser and Norman says, "I don't need that," the teacher can suggest to him how he might respond: "Betty did that because she likes you. Get the eraser from her and say thank you." When the boy asks Norman's opinion of his cartoon and Norman has no reply, the teacher can prompt gently, "He likes you, that's why he's asking your opinion."

Later, if Norman follows through on a gentle prompt (and they shouldn't be so frequent that they become aversive; no one likes nagging), his teacher or parents have a positive, making-friends behavior to build on, with their praise and encouragement and enjoyable time.

In helping a child learn behavior that brings other children closer instead of driving them away, it's again important to remember that the changing of old patterns isn't something that happens instantaneously. A child isn't going to gather a house full of friends around him overnight. He isn't going to get over being shy right away; he has to learn first, through praise and encouragement, that he's a worthwhile person whom others want to be with.

Negative behaviors don't spring full-blown from the conscious mind of a six-year-old; neither do the kinds of behavior that involve other children. Friendships, even among young people, require small, thoughtful, winning gestures between people to build the bonds of affection and caring. It also takes small negative actions to drive them away. Parents have to be aware of what is happening when they see their children without friends, and once they begin to encourage positive, making-friends behaviors, they have to believe that something is going on quietly, bit by bit, and that it's worth the effort.

Behavior toward friends in childhood is something a person carries through a whole lifetime. Having friends bolsters the idea that "I am a worthwhile person . . . because people out there in the world want to be with me." What a pity if a child is cut off from that kind of satisfaction because caring behaviors aren't given room to grow within the family and without.

Happiness for your child isn't a matter of luck, but of being aware of what is going on in the child's life and how his behavior is helping or hindering the image he has of himself, and the image others have of him.

The child who feels worthless, unpraised, or, worse, heavily criticized may find his satisfactions by withdrawing, being shy, so that his self-image is protected from further damage.

The child who is aggressive and demanding is going to go through life trying to bring people closer in inappropriate ways.

The child who has friends is going to feel good about himself—and be a happy child.

Chapter Eleven

WHAT DOES IT MEAN TO BE GROWN-UP?

"Raising children" is an apt and vivid description of what we try to do as parents: literally and metaphorically raising them up out of the cradle and pointing them toward adulthood with a repertoire of useful behaviors and social skills reflecting our own experience, beliefs, and understanding.

By the time children have been "raised," it's expected that they will be independent individuals capable of going out and surviving happily in the world, who most likely will want to raise children of their own to become independent human beings capable of finding satisfaction in the world . . . and on and on. The march of generations carries our values and attitudes and those of our ancestors through the behavior of our offspring—and theirs, and theirs . . .

WHAT'S AN ADULT?

Any parent knows that growing up is not an easy process—but many of us know as well that it doesn't always need to be full of turmoil and crisis. It's a matter of understanding, defining, and then encouraging what it really means to be grown-up. Since our society has no universal rite of passage for the transition from childhood to adulthood, we tend to define grown-upness in terms of specific empowerments and privileges such as driving a car, wearing makeup, going out on dates, being allowed to vote or drink. One of the ways our children get into trouble is when we define the transition in terms of behavior that cannot be called positive.

All of us know of children who define grown-upness as being hard, violent, destructive, and uncaring, just as we know of adults who convey their so-called maturity by being sharp operators, authoritarians, cool, detached, and cynical. Yet when parents are asked what they wish to see in their children as representative of being grown-up, the great majority stress the positive social values of self-reliance, caring, and responsibility.

Taken together with the competing negative traits that also define being grown-up for some, these characteristics comprise the heads or tails of childhood's transitional choices. Parents can't expect their children to decide automatically in favor of the kinder, gentler, more responsible view of maturity, because peer pressure, the daily newspapers, and half the things they see on television urge otherwise. True grown-up behavior has to be taught, both in words and by the parents modeling actions that demonstrate independence, caring, and responsibility.

To that end, there are two classes of behavior that cannot be nurtured too early. The ability to take disappointment calmly is both a major coping skill and an important sign of maturity. The other can be either sibling caring or Mother Theresa behavior—the classes of behavior that are respectful of the needs, feelings, and wishes of other people. Some years ago, there was a popular self-help book for parents called *The Hurried Child*, which cautioned parents against robbing their offspring of childhood by forcing them to become little adults. On the contrary, nurturing the ability to handle disappointment calmly and to be caring of the interests of others will only add to the richness and satisfaction of childhood and lay a solid base for a successful adult life to follow.

"YOU CAN'T MAKE ME!"

The seeds of independence exist at a very young age, with the first step a baby takes, with the proud achievements of learning to tie shoes or get dressed on one's own. And these kinds of growing-up, independent behaviors are given praise and encouragement as a matter of course. Unfortunately, in the steps away from total dependence on parents, not all independent behaviors are equally praised, or even recognized. And often enough in growing up, children will express their need for independence in inappropriate ways.

None of us travels the road to adulthood, especially the bumpy parts, at a steady speed or in one long glide. The normal and natural efforts of a child to assert independence can come in giant steps, in noticeable positive kinds of behavior, as well as in small, less noticeable but still positive ways. The will to be independent of parents, to be a separate person, can show itself also in defiance, in statements that say, on the surface, "I won't do that, you can't make me"—and mean, "I'm grown-up, you can't tell me what to do anymore."

It may be the principle business of growing up to resolve the tension between parent and child in the quest for independence. But sometimes that tension gets out of hand and escalates to open war between children and their parents, a turn of events that is both unnecessary and unproductive.

This is further complicated by the unfortunate fad of regarding children who defy their parents as disturbed by something, their defiance being seen as a symptom of inner problems that have to be uncovered and solved, even though the same process is repeated in endless permutations all about us in the natural world. The chick pecking its way out of an egg or the butterfly emerging from its cocoon is earning its freedom, and its strength, through struggle. Defiant behavior toward parents and other adults who have some authority over children is an expression of the need for individuality and independence.

However, as in everything else, there are limits to what is acceptable or even tolerable. Children who are extravagantly or perpetually defiant cannot be ignored, and if their struggle is to teach them anything, it has to include an appreciation of consequences.

"My child is going to be a juvenile delinquent." A parent worries when doors are slammed in anger by a defiant child or when harsh words that seem to be saying, "I'm going to have my way, like it or not!" are exchanged. Occasionally, strivings to be independent go so far astray that words are replaced by risky or destructive actions.

A MATTER OF FOCUS

More often than not, the point where this process of individuation becomes troubling is where the parents begin to center their attention in the wrong place. They focus on actions or words that trouble them, ignoring everything else in their child's life, and it goes downhill from there. The only way the parents show they're listening is through expressions of shock, outrage, disappointment, pain.

The child isn't necessarily happy with that result because even though he can't always put his finger on what's wrong, it's producing the wrong kind of separation. But, hey, it's an audience and the show must go on, so Junior keeps testing his parents' reflexes by continually pushing the limits. In the course of striving to simultaneously fulfill and refute their judgement of him, the only thing he's really learning is the habit of defiance.

For some parents, "My child is growing up" has subtler nuances, of a different kind. A child growing up is a reminder that parents are seeing their own years slip by and soon enough the child will be an adult and separate, and all of their lives will change. Most parents do want to see their children become mature, responsible adults; their resistance to the inevitable can be made less painful or more fulfilling by seeing that grown-upness is defined in ways that include the real attributes of maturity: responsibility, caring, concern for others, independence, and bonds of enduring affection between parents and children that are not broken simply because a child steps out into the adult world. Part of our role as parents is preparing our children for adulthood. And if we teach our children well, we will not lose them.

Still, there are moments of testing, of saying in so many words, "Remember, I'm not a little kid, I'm grown-up." The push and pull in a household as children grow toward independence can create strains that sometimes are horrendous. The point is not to make the defiance worthwhile in terms of its negative payoff, which can be extremely damaging to the child's feelings of self-worth and the bonds of caring between parents and child. Nor is the way out to give in to the defiance, which is, in effect, giving the child his own way.

We've seen in the case of Gregory how at a very young age a child had learned to get his own way by pressing the issue to a point where his mother, in despair, let him have whatever he asked for. Not just once, unfortunately, but over and over again, until this learned behavior was an ingrained part of him—and the learning of positive new behaviors required considerable hard work by everyone in the family.

FATHER KNOWS BEST?
CHILDREN KNOW BETTER

Taken in themselves, moments of defiance can seem trivial. Parents want one thing: what they think is best for a child. The child wants another, because he or she thinks, "I know what's best. I'm grown-up enough to make my own decisions."

"I want to ride my bike into town to see Joe," a nine-year-old says.

"You can't, it's too dangerous. When you're older—"

"But I know the rules; I'm careful. I am big enough."

Maybe he takes his bike and goes anyhow, which guarantees another unpleasant time when he's found out. Maybe he doesn't go but spends the afternoon in further arguments—the kind of nagging that gets a response: exasperated, angry, impatient, but a response nonetheless.

Kathy says, "I want to spend the five dollars Grandma gave me for my birthday; she said I could."

"You have to save it," Mother says, "or I'll buy something for you with it."

"But it's mine, I'm eight, I know what I want."

"You're not big enough to decide."

Mother thinks she's being reasonable, Kathy thinks she's being treated like a little child. The result is two unhappy people, each determined to have her way, with Kathy more determined than ever to prove she's grown-up. Her way of proof, however, won't necessarily be a positive one, but one expressed in terms of defiance.

"Why can't I stay up later? I'm big enough."

"No you're not. You go to bed now."

"I won't, and you can't make me."

Continued discussion, reasoning, or arguing will make defiance at bedtime an expected occurrence, a regular battle, time-consuming, and unpleasant.

These are small disputes, with the child trying to exert influence and prove grown-upness in ways that really have nothing to do with being mature. If they continue to be replayed day after day, they establish even more negative kinds of behavior that pass for being grown-up and have far-reaching, destructive results. In the cases mentioned, it has to be considered whether it is worthwhile to say no to a child in relation to what he or she is trying to indicate: "I am a grown-up, separate person."

If bike riding really is too dangerous, no is sufficient, for parents have to be concerned about questions of safety. But if Charles is a careful boy, what is the real value of letting him prove he can go to Joe's house and back safely? Is it really important that Kathy learn saving habits with her birthday gift? Or should she be allowed to show how grown-up she is by choosing something at the store? If it's time to go to bed, then it's time. "You can't make me" deserves no answer, and no arguments. If the child doesn't go to bed, he doesn't, but attention for not going to bed should be minimal.

Twelve-year-old Jerry comes down in the morning, already late for his paper route and too late, he claims, to eat breakfast before he goes out.

"Sit down and eat your breakfast," his father says.

"I don't have time. I'll have some scrambled eggs when I get back if there's time before school."

"You're having your breakfast now, and you're not going to mess up the kitchen again later."

"Oh, Dad, I can't do it. I've got to deliver the papers."

"You should have thought of that when you were lying up there late in bed."

"I just overslept a little, and you don't have to keep telling me what to do."

What Dad is saying to Jerry is, "You're a child, I have to oversee everything you do, and you're going to do things my way."

What Jerry is saying is, "I'm grown-up enough to make my own decisions about when I'm going to eat, and how I'm going to take care of my responsibilities like the paper route."

It's a mild argument, to be sure, but if it happens every day, if no one acknowledges anything about Jerry's abilities to be grown-up and independent, capable of making decisions on his own, Jerry's feelings of self-worth will be diminished. He won't see himself as an independent, worthwhile person, but as one who his father thinks can't take anything upon himself. While it may be true that Jerry's father is annoyed by his habit of oversleeping and being late for breakfast and the paper route, it's not worth an argument, let alone a battle. Parents should learn to choose the battles that are worth fighting, and to avoid being sucked into ones that aren't.

It's worth noting, too, that habitual minor disputes contribute to the process of developing strong feelings of anger toward the parents who won't see a child as grown-up. If the tension continues, Jerry will eventually want to avoid being with his father as much as possible. It's the beginning of a chain reaction, with Jerry's mother being drawn into it on one side or the other, and Jerry himself will be out to prove over and over again, in ways that may well be inappropriate, that he really is an independent person. In these terms, an "independent" person may be, to Jerry, one who defies his parents and stays out late, or never shows up for meals, or hangs around with kids who define independence in the same ways and get into trouble for it. It's far more productive and valuable to encourage behavior that really is grown-up and independent. It is going to happen anyhow, the fact of growing up, and parents have a responsibility to teach those behaviors that indicate true maturity and responsibility from an early age.

ASSISTED VISION

In Jerry's case, both his mother and father must help him learn to feel good about himself as a separate, independent, responsible human being. They have to encourage those behaviors that will confirm to him that he's grown-up enough to make his own decisions about when to eat and when to deliver the papers. His parents have to learn to see the *specific* things Jerry does that show grown-upness and a sense of responsibility, and then encourage that kind of behavior with their praise and approval.

For example, Jerry does get up every morning for his paper route. It doesn't matter that his father says, "I had a paper route when I was a kid, all boys do," or that Jerry does it to earn money to buy a new bike, or for any other motivation. It doesn't matter that he's been doing it for months, and it's so routine now that no one thinks twice about it, that it's an expected activity on Jerry's part.

It *does* matter, though, that it's a grown-up and responsible job. Jerry needs to be reminded of that with praise and communication of the idea that taking on a job, handling money, seeing it's done on time, doing it even when the weather's bad or he has something he'd rather do, all indicate real maturity.

There are plenty of occasions when the striving to be more grown-up can either be passed over in silence or acknowledged and encouraged. When I've worked with parents on this problem of defiance and shown how it is an expression of a child's wanting to be independent and separate, it's surprising what a list of positive grown-up behaviors they can come up with, things they've learned to see just by paying a little more attention:

Helped his father paint the fence.

Tried eating asparagus for the first time.

Fed the dog.

Closed all the windows during a rainstorm while I was away.

Came home exactly at time promised.

Brought books home from school for a friend who was sick.

Responsible behaviors ought to be rewarded with praise as a way of teaching young children those behaviors you value. And remember that the child who is made to feel good about himself for behaving in a grown-up and responsible manner is more likely to be the teenager out in a much wider world who comes home from dates on time, understands the responsibilities of driving safely, knows how to judge the decisions he or she is called on to make in situations other than the home, reflects the positive values parents have tried to teach rather than the phony separateness and independence that often take the form of defiant behaviors.

CHARACTER, FATE, AND MARSHMALLOWS

Growing up successfully depends on skills that are a lot different from simply being compliant with parents' wishes. Rewards for compliance are pretty close to rewards for nonbehavior—the child who is praised for nothing at all: "You're so good, I didn't know you were there." We don't want to teach our children to be robots, nor do we want them to make no waves at all. A human being who simply says yes to everything may have no conflicts, but will have very few real rewards from life in the outside world.

Sometimes, as Nancy Reagan never tired of reminding us, the best rewards in life can come from just saying no. A case in point involves a group of four-year-olds who were subjects of a study some years ago that dealt with the age-old problem of temptation. Happily, in this case, the desired object was not drugs or cigarettes or alcohol but a marshmallow.

What the researchers were looking for were clues to child-hood personality characteristics related to the subject's ability to earn rewards through delayed gratification. For adults, delayed gratification can mean things like not buying a new car until you can afford at least a down payment, not having sex until you have negotiated the consent of your partner, and waiting until you've earned the necessary points for a real vacation before cashing in your frequent flier plan. For the children in the study, it meant a double-or-nothing deal on sweets.

The researcher met with each subject individually, then said he had to step out of the room for a short errand. Before he left, he placed a marshmallow on the table as a gift. If the child wanted to eat it, he was told, he could have it right away; on the other hand, if he wanted to wait until after the fake errand, when the researcher returned he would give him a second marshmallow and he then could have them both. The only way to get the second one was by waiting.

A few of the children didn't even wait for him to get out the door. Some of the rest agonized for a few seconds or even a few minutes before grabbing the prize from the table and popping it into their mouth. Still others fought an heroic battle for self-control, doing everything they could think of to keep themselves from losing the reward—examining their shoes, pacing in circles around the table, wringing their hands, looking at the ceiling. It wasn't about who liked marshmallows and who didn't. It was about who could control his or her appetite and put off satisfying the immediate desires in a trade-off for twice the reward later.

For the psychologists who ran the study as well as some of the children who were in it, the big payoff came later. Several years after the initial experiment, the researchers followed up with their subjects, who were now about to graduate from high school. What they found was that those who had demonstrated the greatest amount of impulse control when they were four were still using those same skills as teenagers, and still reaping the rewards. They were far better students, better adjusted socially, better focused on long-term goals, and far more decisive than their peers who had opted for the bird in hand.

The evaluations were not just subjective; the children who had waited for their reward scored an astonishing 210 points higher on their SATs—with 610 on verbal and 652 on quantitative—than their hastier counterparts.

Impulse control is not an instinct, and so far there's not much evidence that it's imprinted on our genes. Whatever our legacy, there is no doubt that for the most part it's one of those things we learn from our parents—and, like every other social skill, we either learn it well, moderately, poorly, or hardly at all.

Successful parents know how to teach impulse control. They demonstrate the skills at home and at work and nurture them in their children through teaching them how to take disappointment calmly (see Chapter 6).

Most of the time, when you see a child who can't control his temper, whether you read about him in the newspaper or if he's sitting across from you at the dinner table, it's because his parents haven't shown him how.

Teaching responsible, successful independent behavior means that you are giving your child a way of behaving in the world that will enable him or her to deal with the problems and challenges of adolescent and adult life, to be a person less influenced by the pull of others because he has a strong, internal set of values to guide his behavior and help him make his own decisions.

And he ought to collect a few marshmallows along the way.

Chapter Twelve

CHORES THAT TEACH . . . RESENTMENT

How do you teach your child that all-important attribute of maturity, a sense of responsibility?

Being a responsible person is as valued a form of behavior in the adult world as it is in family life, and the ability to assume responsibility is something that is learned in the process of growing up—if the child is taught appropriately.

Responsibility and reliability are very often the most noteworthy qualities about people one works with or knows on a basis less intimate than friendship.

"He's not a very friendly guy," people will say, "but he does do his job."

"She's not someone it's easy to get close to, but you can rely on her."

More often than not, the person who has a sense of responsibility that is recognized by others is someone people like to have around. A person you can trust is a person you want as a friend. The charming, unreliable rogues of fiction and real life are memorable, but few parents want their children to grow up to be like them.

Teaching responsible behavior begins early, like the teaching of other kinds of behavior. Responsibility, like happiness, is open to many interpretations. It shouldn't mean compliancy. And it is not simply a question of completing a checklist of tasks, although many parents seem to feel that this is the way to teach children responsibility.

CHORES AND CONFLICTS

Doing chores—a common enough necessity in many households—is not the way to teach a child how to be responsible, especially if the chore requirement takes on the nature of a battle.

"You're going to do this job whether you like it or not, young man, and you have no choice in the matter" doesn't do much for the relationship between parents and child. The occasion is more likely to be one where the child uses a stubborn refusal to defy his parents and show how independent he is.

I have found, in fact, that parents who have children with the most behavioral problems are often the ones who give them the most chores, the long lists of things to be done at certain times.

"It teaches them responsibility," those parents are quick to protest. "They learn . . . they learn . . ."

Yes, but what do they learn? They learn that a parent has decided what chores they are going to do, and if they don't get them done, they may be facing a long quarrel, anger, exasperation, even some kind of punishment.

Frequently such parents know there's something not quite right about the system they've tried to impose on the family, if for no other reason than that they're asking their children to do chores that they themselves don't especially enjoy doing. Some, although not all, will admit to themselves at least that chores are one way of getting work done. If they have any guilt about giving a lot of chores, they fall back on the "responsibility" argument.

"Everybody has to learn to do things they don't like to do."

"How else can I teach Lennie responsibility if I don't give chores?"

It's as if washing a floor, taking out the trash, or cleaning up a room on a regular schedule will somehow help prepare a child to become an adult. Yet the world is full of people who as children never made their beds, never mowed a lawn, never dried the dishes, and nevertheless grew up to be responsible adults. I offer as an example my own childhood, which was never darkened by a single assigned chore.

The one sure result of a program of chores for children who resist the whole idea is children who resent their parents and who get involved in constant disputes about why chores weren't done. There is nothing wrong and there are many things right about a child contributing to the work of the household. Many children will help spontaneously because they wish to imitate their parents, or because other forms of encouraging responsibility for the well-being of the family give them a push toward less pleasant tasks. If it comes about peacefully, that's wonderful. If, however, in order to have children do their share, you find yourself on a perpetual battlefield, you may be paying too high a price to have clothes hung up, the table set, or the toys returned to their proper place.

The price you may be paying is the immediate stress of making that chore get done and the less-apparent, long-range consequence of raising a child who wants to get as far away from home as soon as possible.

Mrs. Harris talked about the difficulties of her situation, raising five children between the ages of eleven and nineteen. She said she had been widowed a few years earlier, when the youngest boy was about seven, and she had returned to full-time work as a dietician at a local school.

"I have to rely on the children to do chores," she said. "I just don't have the time to do the laundry and the housecleaning, the dishes and the cooking, and work at my job as well. They have to pitch in and help out. Of course, even before their father died, we gave them chores to do. The girls each had their tasks around the house from the time they were little, and the boys helped out, too. But even back then, there was never a time when they didn't resist every step of the way. We couldn't seem to make them understand that this was the kind of thing they'd have to do when they were grown-up, so it was good for them to learn to take on responsibilities now.

"It's gotten out of hand, and now trying to get them to do things is making all of our lives unpleasant. And I feel guilty that they don't have a father and I have to be away so much of the day at work."

Mrs. Harris had lists all over the place, about who should do what when, and just about every item on those lists represented a potential scene or conflict.

The problem was not that she needed help in running the household and wasn't getting it. The problem was that she was confusing chores with responsibility, and paying too high a price in terms of the gradual destruction of the bonds between herself and her children just to get chores done. Doing chores per se is not grown-up behavior, but understanding why chores need to be done is. Mrs. Harris was looking at lists instead of seeing her children.

"I've lost my two oldest girls," she said. "Both of them are engaged or close to it. They're still living at home, but you couldn't guess it from the time they spend there. The people they're close to are their fiancés' families. The younger one even cooks dinner over at their place, and the older of the two is relying on the boy's mother for advice about the wedding."

The three youngest children?

"Well, yes, I still have them doing their chores, and the two big girls, too, when I can get them to."

Any problems with the young ones?

"You know how kids are, it's a constant struggle to get them just to take out the trash and take their proper turns doing dishes. Yes, I guess you could say that getting chores done always means some kind of fight. Nobody does them willingly."

Does Mrs. Harris realize the true price she's paid by assigning chores whose main goals are to nurture her children's character? Two daughters making every effort to separate themselves from her, three younger children who could easily be doing the same as early as possible?

"Life means responsibility," Mrs. Harris protests. "How else do you teach them?"

Life and being a parent also mean closeness and caring. What a parent wants to encourage in the parent-child relationship is love. Nobody loves his Top Sergeant; forced "responsibility" is a sentence, not a sharing of the tasks that keep a home running smoothly.

PETS AND RESPONSIBILITY

Another form of "teaching responsibility" that's common and probably equally as unproductive as lists of chores is the chain of events that starts with, "Let's get the child a puppy to teach her to be responsible." I wonder how many dogs and kittens end up being the total responsibility of the parents as soon as the novelty wears off. Who feeds the pet, walks it, cleans up after it? And what has become of the lesson in responsibility it was supposed to teach? A child who doesn't take pride in being responsible simply because such behavior is approved of isn't going to become responsible because he suddenly has a dog to take care of, just as a child who's friendless isn't going to make friends just by being sent to camp and put in touch with a lot of other kids.

Responsible behavior is the product of praise and nurture for being grown-up, for acting in ways that show independence. Simply putting the dirty clothes in the washing machine isn't anything more than a mechanical action, but the parent's recognition and praise makes the chore worthwhile and a source of self-pride. Helping when you're needed is grown-up; the specific task is unimportant, but too many parents see the task done or undone before they see what it represents.

WHAT'S THE REAL GOAL?

The ability to teach responsibility depends first of all on seeing the small but valuable grown-up actions all children do from time to time, and then giving those actions positive recognition, so that the child will repeat them, or similar actions, because being grown-up brings parental approval.

Sharon has gone down the street to play with a friend. Before she left, her mother said, "Be home by five o'clock, Sharon," and Sharon promises that she will be.

She's home promptly at five. Wisely, although it was expected behavior, her mother praises the six-year-old for doing what she had promised, a natural variation on the ABCD nurture response.

"It was responsible of you to come home on time," her mother says. "I like to see you doing that."

The little pieces of the whole picture of being grown-up and responsible are put together as Sharon gets older. She takes good telephone messages; that's grown-up. She volunteers to help set the table. It may be simply a question of imitating what Mother does, but it's a job grown-ups have to do, so her mother praises her for helping—and when, in the future, Mother asks Sharon to set the table, it's not a chore that has to be done, it's the grown-up thing to do. In years to come, when Sharon is a teenager going out in the evening and she's told to be home at a certain hour, it's mature and responsible for her to do so, not a requirement that is there to be circumvented if possible.

"Clean up your room, how can you stand this mess?"

For some children, cleaning up isn't all that important.

"I don't want to."

"Well, I want you to, and you have half an hour to do it. Grown-ups have to clean up after themselves."

Somehow it doesn't make being grown-up so valuable—being responsible for having an orderly room or a bed that's made first thing in the morning—if it's put in those terms. On the other hand, a parent who doesn't make the neat room or the made bed an issue between parent and child isn't going to suffer the strain of constant disputes. "You will" and "No, I won't" are about as far as the argument should go, lest the appeal of a lot of attention over the messy room, or whatever the chore in question, overshadows either the benefits of getting it done or the parent's satisfaction in being obeyed.

The fact is, a parent's words are heard; the child knows that the chore under discussion is something that the parent wants, and one day the room gets cleaned up beautifully, with all the toys and books in their proper places. Now is the time for praise, for communicating values, for making the connection between doing a chore and being grown-up and responsible.

"You did a terrific job cleaning up your room. It pleases me to see you taking care of your things. That's very grown-up."

There are a lot of myths about how to teach values, and one that does a good deal of harm to the relationship between parents and children is that work—obeying orders—will make a child into a responsible adult. Unfortunately, it's one of those magic formulas for behavior that just doesn't work. It exacts a high price in many cases because of the opposition it can create.

Don't get me wrong about the value of doing things for others. Caring for another human being, making life easier for Mother, respecting the needs, wishes, and feelings of friends or strangers—all those things are praiseworthy behavior and indications of being mature and grown-up. But if these behaviors don't come from the child—if they are forced on him by a parent—there's a good chance they'll slow down the growth process and build more resentment than character.

Praise builds responsibility, and to praise you must see and encourage the quiet attitudes and actions that are responsible behavior patterns in miniature. Lists and assignments aren't enough, not if the price you pay is a weakening of the bonds of caring between you and your child.

Chapter Thirteen

IT'S GROWN-UP
TO BE CARING

"I want Alison to grow up to be a happy person who cares about other people as much as she cares about herself. It seems to me that both things are terribly important."

Alison's mother is right. Among the least-stressed, most-overlooked qualities of maturity are genuine sensitivity and caring for others—sibling caring, Mother Theresa behavior, and taking disappointment calmly. We hear a lot, maybe too much, in the media about "sensitivity" and "emotional bonding" and the like for people who are suddenly worried that maybe they don't have them. Promoters who develop sensitivity-training techniques have a field day with the subject because it's so abstract that it can mean whatever they want it to. It can give rise to opportunities for "talking it out," hours of therapy to set emotions free, and "getting in touch" with your feelings and the feelings of others. It has become a lucrative occupation for the variety of advisers who claim to guide men and women to learn how to be sensitive.

Sometimes these self-help programs and associated forms of therapy work, but often they don't. No parents, though, want to believe that this is what the future holds for their children—a sense of emotional incapacity that has to be corrected. They want, like Alison's mother, to have their children acquire a sense of caring as part of the process of growing up.

WHAT IS CARING BEHAVIOR?

What parents often don't realize is that the caring behavior they're talking about is a kind of positive behavior that is teachable at a young age, and that is related to all the other behaviors on which they place high value.

A caring child or adult has friends.

She has a good self-image; she knows she does things that others think are worthwhile, and therefore she is worthwhile.

A responsible child or adult cares about the effect of her actions on other people. They, in turn, trust her.

Part of independent behavior is being aware of one's actions in relation to others, sensitivity about how a certain kind of behavior is going to affect another person—it's the quality Dr. Daniel Goleman refers to as emotional intelligence.

The bonds of love between parents and children that flourish in an atmosphere of praise, in environments that feel good, are extended in later years to friends, to spouses, to children.

The rate of divorce in this country is now approaching 50 percent, and how many times the grounds are cited as incompatibility or cruelty or irreconcilable differences. These phrases of the law very often simply define a lack of caring and sensitivity, the fact that people often find it difficult to show or even to feel genuine bonds of affection for others.

Even when a husband and wife, for example, do "care," they may never have learned how to give and take, how to see caring behavior when it's being shown—just as some parents cannot see quiet behavior in their children.

In our world it is far too common to view things negatively, the kind of negative scanning that makes parents see only what is not right and ignore what is right. We are confronted again by the model for life that focuses on the disease, the problem, instead of on health and problem-free living.

You can teach your children caring behavior. You can take a child who seems to have little sense of what caring about others means and give him or her a foundation for happiness that is perhaps one of the most significant aspects of being "grown-up."

CARING SHOULD BE TAUGHT AT HOME

The things that signify caring in our society are different for different people. Very often between adults, married couples, for example, caring behavior can be a lot of small things they do for each other. In fact, Dr. Richard Stuart, who works with couples who have marital problems, has a system of "caring days" where couples make an effort to build a good, caring relationship by doing just those little things that signify caring to each spouse.

We can build this attribute of adulthood in our children by teaching them to be caring when they are young. It's a matter of creating that positive feeling of self-worth in them, so that they are easily able to build the self-worth of others.

We call it "thoughtfulness," an important caring behavior that has wide implications in the grown-up world, where the reward for a thoughtful, caring response to others is close bonds between friends and associates, between spouses, and with one's children.

"Isn't that cute," we say of children who do something thoughtful spontaneously. But it's more than cute, and we should be heavily praising the child who calls a sick friend to see how he is or tells another that she's really sorry she can't come over but be sure to call again tomorrow. Sharing is thoughtful, a gesture like picking flowers for Mother or all the little things children do that show they are not just thinking of themselves but are sensitive to the feelings and needs of others. Sibling caring is a part of the natural bond, but it is the parent whose eyes see this and other caring behaviors and who nurtures them.

We teach children with praise, with labeling the many different actions as valuable. It's part of the job of being a parent, whether or not you yourself are especially caring and thoughtful, to teach your children what it means. It's a lot less expensive than raising children who don't know how to care and end up as adults who search for answers about how to make people like them, how to express what they feel for others.

Rick's teacher noticed his lack of sensitivity for the feelings of his classmates in the fifth grade. In an attempt to be funny, he would say things like "You look like a monkey," or "You can only play backstop" to a heavy boy during a recess baseball game. If the other kids laugh at his insensitive comments, he gains a slight feeling of self-worth. When he finds fault with other children, he increases his feelings of self-worth at the expense of others— by making others look inferior, Rick feels superior to them or that he has balanced his own shortcomings.

Rick's parents, and his teacher on occasion, have tried to change Rick's behavior, to make him more sensitive to the feelings of others.

"We've reasoned with him. We've asked him how he would feel if the shoe were on the other foot and people said those kinds of things about him. We've asked him time and time again why he says these things. Nothing does any good. It's as if he doesn't hear us, he only hears those kind of embarrassed laughs he gets from the other kids."

Those laughs are a distorted form of praise for Rick, even if the kids themselves are slightly uncomfortable about it. His insensitivity results in people paying attention to him.

SILENT NURTURE

The way to teach Rick more sensitive behavior is not to talk about it, because the criticism implied by recounting what Rick has done wrong ensures that he's not listening. It's the nonteachable moment, and more effective in teaching Rick is a brief, immediate reprimand: "I don't like what I hear. I don't want you to talk that way to anyone." He knows, without discussion, that his behavior isn't appropriate.

The process for teaching more sensitive behavior is the same as previously outlined: praise, communication of values in the teachable moment following praise, and an extra reward in terms of enjoyable time. Praise for the smallest incidents that show sensitivity, whether or not Rick really feels caring: a moment of sharing, a comment that builds up another child rather than tearing him down, a gesture that shows Rick is thinking of the other person—Mother Theresa behavior, which indicates both emotional maturity and emotional intelligence.

In teaching caring behavior, we help build self-esteem, and if a child feels good about herself, she'll find it easy to care about how her friends feel. Caring behavior reaches years into the future.

Parents can teach caring by recognizing it and making it as valuable to the child as it is to them. It is an important lesson in becoming grown-up, and the ability to reach out and respond to others with sensitivity and understanding is something even the youngest child can begin to develop as a positive behavior that will last a lifetime.

Chapter Fourteen

LEARNING TO LEARN

A child with problems at school gets lots of attention, not only from parents but also from teachers and classmates, administrators and counselors.

For parents, even the earliest academic or behavioral problems at school can appear to have enormous consequence. The development of a child's personality and character, the beginning of a reputation and indeed even a resume, the chances for higher education, a choice of careers, the ability to compete in the marketplace as adults—all these are related in the parent's mind to how successfully their children negotiate their first real venture into the outside world, and how well or how poorly they adjust to learning.

Recently, too, we have been handed a great deal of information and speculation about learning problems—those of the so-called learning-disabled child, the hyperactive child, even the gifted child—and how to "cure" them, which implies again that children's behavior has as its source a problem somewhere deep inside. Educators and psychologists often devote their careers to finding and exorcising the demons that seem to be hindering the learning process.

But learning, or resistance to it, is a behavior like any other, and positive learning-related behaviors, from wanting or being able to read to paying attention in the classroom, in large part must be taught. Parents have as much responsibility to encourage and nourish thirst-for-learning behaviors as they do a sense of responsibility, making-friends behavior, and all the positive behaviors we have discussed. When something is holding a child back or causing him to be disruptive in the classroom, or makes him resist going to school, it is defeatist and irresponsible to cede the child's entire future to a faulty behavior pattern or a neurological deficit. Annie Sullivan would be the first to tell you that the focus has to be on the behavior itself: exactly what it is, how it can be corrected, and how to nurture *any* child's natural thirst for learning.

SMALL BEGINNINGS

Where does that thirst for learning come from? What makes a child like to learn or want to read? Consider how much of what we know derives from our ability to understand the written word, especially nowadays, in the new age of electronic communication of information and entertainment. You can't operate a computer, send or receive e-mail or a fax, or even responsibly maintain a bank account unless you know how to read. Whatever the future may bring, the chances are that technology will continue to increase, rather than reduce, the percentage of our knowledge we obtain from writing.

The inability to read well is at the bottom of most learning difficulties.

Parents are often heard to say, "She never stops talking," or "We can hardly shut him up." Not too many say, "That child never stops reading." Talking, of course, is fun and it gets an immediate response. While many children do find reading fun, the skill is less likely to produce similar gratification from the world beyond the printed page, certainly not in the same immediate way and often not until long after the habit of reading is well established.

Again, our behavior comes back to consequences. The consequence of learning to speak words and the consequence of learning to read them are quite different. These two kinds of learned behavior are given different responses by parents. Just learning to say "Mama" provokes a lot of attention, hugs, smiles, encouragement to say it again, to say new words. But it's another matter when a child of four or five begins to figure out that those black squiggles on a page are the symbols for words and sentences and objects and ideas. For one thing, it's usually not a single event that produces a spectacular response like the first "Mama," and in most households it is followed by few immediate consequences. Conversely, people will start paying a lot more notice to a child when such a milestone is missed than when it is achieved. When a child should be able to read but cannot, or doesn't like to learn in school, or won't pay attention, it is usually because these skills and behaviors have not been properly nurtured. The attention the child gets following the discovery of such a deficit can send a powerfully negative message and is often of the wrong kind.

It may be even more distressing to the parents. "But we read all the time," they will say. "There are books all over the house."

Again, imitation is not a reliable way to encourage behavior. Teaching by example, communicating the value of learning simply by being a learning-oriented parent, sets a nice tone, but it may not have much effect on whether a child acquires the same behavior. At best, it provides a little extra incentive for the child who wants to be like Mom and Dad.

On the other hand, parents can provide the same encouragement for learning—even for the most fundamental learning skill, reading—as they offer in the normal course of growing up for speaking: immediate positive consequences. They can give a child a thirst for learning before he reaches the highly complex process of formal education.

It must be pointed out that there is a distinction between teaching behaviors such as responsibility, being a better friend, being independent and grown-up, and teaching thirst-for-learning behaviors. A making-friends behavior, for example, is relatively isolated and, when present, exists within fairly narrow limits, so while a lack of friends may have an effect on the child's life, it's fairly easy for parents to encourage or discourage actions within that class of behavior. When we speak of formal education, however, we are dealing with a far more complex structure of learning, with a variety of prerequisites if a child is to make progress. Reading and math are taught step-by-step, and if the child misses out on a step, he can't successfully go on to the next. Parents can't ordinarily provide the missing parts, however much help they want to give with homework. Formal education, in the long run, must be in the hands of professionals.

What does rest with the parents, however, is the basis for that thirst for learning. They can provide the kind of nurture that sets the stage for the formal process that begins when a child enters school, and that makes it all worthwhile.

PUTTING HONEY ON THE LETTERS: THE SCHOOL CONTRACT

An expressive model of how parents can nurture an early thirst for learning is provided by a ancient tradition related to teaching the Hebrew alphabet. In the Middle Ages, Jewish boys were given slates on which each letter of the alphabet was coated with honey. The boy licked off the honey and learned the letter; learning was made sweet in a tangible fashion.

We already make speaking sweet by rewarding it with nurture. The parent who wishes to instill an eagerness to learn in a child must remember that reading must be made sweet with nurture, too.

A child making sense out of the black marks on a page in a book—"That means cat!"—deserves as much attention as he did when he spoke his first word. The accomplishment of being able to understand whatever lies beneath the words in writing must be communicated as having great value—and not when the child is already in the midst of a school situation but during preschool years. Don't underestimate the significance of a child translating the squiggles of an *A* or a *B*; it's exactly the same skill that demystified the Rosetta stone and now points mankind toward outer space. Nurturing the use of this essential tool of education is one of the most powerful ways parents have of giving a child a taste of honey and the sweetness of learning.

So many learning problems arise because a child sees no value in reading, because there are few rewards in the early years. When the time comes when rewards are granted by grades on papers, the child who doesn't do well is likely to be burdened with a label that defines his learning abilities for the rest of his life. Before the child ever leaves the home, high value must be placed on the behaviors that will be rewarded in school. Or, stated another way: spare the honey, spoil the child's future.

On occasion, it might be helpful to formulate a school contract between parents and child.

Schools have a contract of their own with the child, of course, backed by a variety of incentives. Grades, for example, allow the parents and teachers to monitor a child's achievement level, but they also provide powerful reinforcement for a student's thirst-for-learning behavior. So do medals, ribbons, gold and silver stars, student-of-the-week or best achiever awards, and a variety of entitlements that can range from hall passes, participation in sports or acting in a theater production, to leading a school parade.

No parents ever send their children to school in the hope that they will become a professional hall monitor or make a career of collecting gold stars. Whatever incentives we choose in support of our child's thirst-for-learning behavior, they are just the first step and soon enough will be replaced by internal rewards. The sense of inner satisfaction is an important part of grown-up life. Whatever other rewards we give our children to start them on the way, the ultimate goal is a feeling of personal delight and worthwhileness, which gives life its meaning and is a powerful motivator to achievement.

Whatever incentive you settle on for your school contract, the only criterion that counts is that it be something of value to your child. Most families use money; it's a motivator in the adult world, it comes in units that easily fit the numerical scoring system in the contract, and it gives them a chance to nurture other useful behaviors such as intelligent decision making on how to save or spend.

The rewards in a school contract are based on four criteria: everyday grades, projects, reading, and monthly averages. Note that there are no debit items, meaning no penalties are subtracted from a child's score for any reason; the cost of below-standard performance is simply that they do not earn points for a particular item. The parents and child agree in advance on the value of points, whether in dollars or another motivator.

SAMPLE CONTRACT

Everyday School Grades	*Points*
C (70–74)	5
C+ (75–79)	10
B (80–84)	25
B+ (85–89)	50
A (90–94)	75
A+ (95 or higher)	100

Projects Completed and Ready to Be Handed In	
On-time	25
24 hours early	100

Project Grades	
B	100
B+	200
A	400
A+	600

Number of Book Assignments Read during Month	
1	100
2	300
3	800
4	1,200

Monthly Number of Grades B+ or Higher

3	500
5	1,000
7	1,500
8	2,000

THE "LEARNING DISABLED" CHILD

"Joey isn't learning in school, he's not achieving," his parents say. "He's in the fourth grade, and we don't think he's made any progress at all since he's been going to school. He's always been an active child, and he doesn't concentrate well, so he doesn't pay attention, and he doesn't learn.

"Of course," they add, "we knew when he first started school that he had a problem. His nursery school teacher told us so, five years ago."

That's a familiar scenario. Faced with an active boy, seemingly quite bright, who doesn't make an effort to learn, the nursery school teacher tells the parents, "Something is causing Joey not to keep up with the other children. He has a problem, a learning disability."

Joey can't learn because he's learning disabled. He's learning disabled because he doesn't learn. The why of one is answered by the why of the other.

Far more likely, Joey's real problem is that he hasn't *learned* to learn. Labeling him as "learning disabled" is like blaming the patient because the doctor doesn't know how to cure the disease.

By the fourth grade his parents and teachers are frustrated.

"He knows something one day in arithmetic, and the next day, or two days later, it's as if he's never heard of it before. He'll learn his spelling words and then almost at once he forgets them. Nothing stays with him."

"He's very unhappy," his mother says. "He has what I'd call a poor self-image, no confidence in himself. He calls himself a dummy, yet we've had neurological examinations and all kinds of tests that don't seem to find anything to explain it. He's had trouble ever since he started school."

Does his mother spend a lot of time with him to help him with schoolwork?

"Oh, yes. We read together and work on homework. In fact, he'll remind me that he has homework so I should allow time to help him. But I feel I have to help him, because he has this problem of being learning disabled."

How does she know?

"They told us, and we can see for ourselves that he's getting nowhere. I know if he does something just a little bit well, he's so much happier. If I can do anything to help him, I have to."

Joey has a problem. It's the mother's responsibility as a parent to do what she can to help him, even though no one is able to explain to her how it can be solved. How, indeed, can it be solved, if it's true that there is some undetectable defect in Joey's brain that has disabled him? But the only evidence of this is that he doesn't learn, he forgets things, he thinks of himself as a "dummy," and he has no confidence in his abilities or himself. Could it be that the problem lies somewhere other than in the wiring of his brain?

MORE PROBLEMS WITH LABELS

At the age of four or so, Joey was given a label that has stuck with him through his school years. Sometimes children are labeled as shy or uncooperative or spoiled, and there's very little they can do to break free of the stigma. And why should they try? Even when the label is disparaging or the message is all negative, children—and far too many adults—believe what they hear. "Learning disabled" may be a somewhat more elusive concept, but the effects are just as damning. Mother and Father and teachers know what it means, and they are in a position to see and respond to learning behavior that confirms the label. They pay attention to the negative behavior and allow the quiet moments, when Joey is learning or showing learning behavior that could be encouraged, to pass unnoticed. Joey has been labeled a special child with special needs; parents and teachers redouble their efforts when they see evidence of his "problem" and give him special treatment. Labels often become a self-fulfilling prophesy; if you describe a child in a certain way long enough, the child will begin to act in the way he or she is described.

Mother sets aside time to help with homework; Joey's teacher puts him in reading groups with other children who have been identified with similar labels and set apart from the mainstream. There is a great deal of parental involvement, and there is far less encouragement for Joey to break out of the behavioral pattern that's been set. It doesn't take long for the whole situation to become a self-fulfilling prophecy: by the fourth grade, Joey is indeed learning disabled. The behavior he *has* learned is not to learn. And more than balancing the payoff in increased parental involvement for having learning problems, there's a big negative result. He's getting left further behind. "I'm *only* in the fourth grade," he is heard to remark. "My mother kept me back a year." He's already helping to polish up a poor self-image, which is going to last him a lifetime.

Educators and psychologists often provide a label for behavior that seems to explain what is happening while in reality it does no such thing. Labeling a child in school learning disabled, by itself, offers nothing at all to help us understand the problem. In many cases it's simply a convenience to the system, far less a useful tool for the child and his family than a trap door beneath their feet. At best, labels are worthless in a practical sense; at worst, they are destructive.

"Learning disabled" tells us nothing more than that the child is having problems with learning. Neither the neurologists who decide there is "minimal brain damage" because they can find no brain damage at all, nor the educators who test ability to learn, nor the psychologists who try to uncover the emotional causes for learning problems have ever used this kind of open label to help solve anything.

By far the most effective approach to learning disabilities, especially those that have been labeled by default, is the one that connects behavior to consequences. It puts the honey on the letters. Reading and other kinds of learning behaviors receive immediate rewards. It can correct and reverse deficient or totally lacking learning behaviors, including those associated with problems of defiance and a lack of friends.

I don't want to suggest that the parents of a student who has fallen behind his classmates in school because of diagnosed learning difficulties will be able, all by themselves, to change their child's learning behavior. In the first place, too much of the difficulty takes place in the school environment, where parents have less influence, and there are many more people involved than in the home. I do suggest, however, that parents of young children who are labeled as learning disabled (or who are set apart with one of the other labels educators use to describe children with learning problems) examine the child's behavior carefully before they accept the label. Nobody can reach a solution until they properly identify the problem.

Despite the many theories about the varied nature of learning disabilities, the only effective treatments are the ones that focus on the behavior and how it developed. In the absence of such focus within the school, parents face a lonely struggle. They can take care to not nurture their child's negative self-image at home, but it's hard to offset the effect when such labels define the child at school.

There's a good chance that Joey learned to be learning disabled because initially he didn't get encouragement for thirst-for-learning behaviors and praise for quiet moments when he first discovered letters or numbers. When his nursery school teacher decided he must be learning disabled, because he couldn't learn even though he had average or above average intelligence, the problem began to affect not only Joey's ideas about himself but those of his parents and his future teachers. He received attention for not learning.

His parents were able to make a small beginning toward helping him out of his problem. They tried to make the label less significant by decreasing their attention, constant help, and visible concern. At the same time, any indication they saw of positive learning behavior, even reading a newspaper headline or leafing through a comic book, was carefully nurtured with praise.

Joey's mother remembered that he came home excited and happy because for that day he had been put in a higher reading group—an opportunity for praise and some rewarding time spent with her. Even a page of homework completed or a neatly written paper, in which the spelling mistakes don't cancel out the effort, could be turned into an occasion for making Joey feel a little more worthwhile—and better able to learn.

In the final analysis, however, the principal burden of dealing with children who have been labeled learning disabled, like the whole process of formal education, has to lie with the professionals. Only a professional can actually teach a child the steps of learning in a formal environment to help him catch up and, one hopes, make learning a rewarding experience. Just don't depend on professionals alone. In most cases it's unlikely that professionals by themselves can bring the child up to grade level. It's tremendously important for parents of preschool children to sweeten the interest in learning as early as possible, even though the ultimate rewards may still seem distant.

THE HYPERACTIVE CHILD AND OTHER PROBLEMS

A few years ago I met with a teacher about a boy in her class who was having trouble learning. I made the decision to speak with her because the parents told me the child had been labeled learning disabled.

The teacher said she had been alerted in advance that the boy had a problem, but knowing what was coming hadn't made it any easier to deal with him when he arrived. She told me he was disruptive in the classroom, talking out loud and refusing to stay in his seat, disturbing the other children and making life miserable for everyone—including her.

She confided in me, "If I didn't know better, I would have said Carl's only problem was that he was obnoxious." But the label of learning disabled required her to overlook the obvious. The problem orientation of modern education had persuaded this teacher, and countless other teachers and parents, to view the Carls of the classroom not as badly behaved children but as children driven by a disorder. If a child is behaving in an obnoxious manner, there is one set of consequences—the very least of which would be to try putting a stop to it. But when identical behavior has an intimidating label like learning disability, the attached consequences are entirely different.

Once labeled, behavior that should justifiably make a parent or teacher angry, for example, now requires solicitous concern, attention, special help—all the kinds of responses that encourage a child to continue offending.

Consider hyperactivity, a current favorite among educators and psychologists as well as medical people who are trying to pin down the "cause." Whatever evidence has been gathered about chemical additives to food, allergies, and nutritional deficiencies as factors contributing to hyperactivity doesn't help a bit in dealing with the actual behavior. And *that's* the problem: most often, the reason inappropriate behavior continues is because the child perceives it as worthwhile. That also may be the key to how it can be reversed.

Some children are more physically active than others, some have shorter attention spans, some have had so little encouragement to read and enjoy learning that thirst-for-learning behavior isn't a part of their behavioral repertoire and few classroom situations can hold their interest. The more unpleasant learning becomes, the more they act out to escape.

"She's hyperactive," an educator or psychologist will say, and indeed, the child in question is less interested in sitting still and paying attention. The label has been applied, and forever after, the behavior is going to be encouraged by the attention that is paid whenever it manifests itself.

Melissa has learned that a certain kind of behavior, which the grown-ups in charge of her label as hyperactivity, will make her the center of concern at home and in the classroom.

"What did you do when her teacher told you Melissa was hyperactive?"

"Our very first thought was 'We've got a problem,'" her parents will say. They will find out what they can about hyperactivity, then use the knowledge to suppress a normal response the next time they see Melissa acting up at the dinner table.

Suddenly, quite predictably, the problem will get much worse. And even though the parents now have a label that describes the behavior, they have been given nothing at all to help Melissa control it.

But there may be an answer, and it has to do with the behavior that is being inadvertently encouraged. When a parent or teacher is disturbed by signs of "hyperactivity," regardless of the cause, they pay attention. And that attention is a reward.

The same pattern can be seen with children who have so-called dyslexia, or who have minor speech problems. A young child learning to read or to speak stumbles over words or writes a letter backward. Parents are immediately concerned; they look for more instances. The label is applied, and time and attention are centered on the problem. There is an immediate payoff for writing letters in the reverse direction or stuttering. It should be remembered that *even if* it is possible to determine some physiological or neurological cause for the difficulties we have been discussing, the repeated additional attention and involvement given such children may inadvertently nurture the negative behavior. It encourages its existence, helps it to grow, teaches the child that it is worthwhile to see letters backward, to stutter, to disrupt home and classroom with excess activity.

Even in cases where children have epileptic seizures, research has shown that a part of the disorder can be operant, which means that the epilepsy responds to positive consequences. When these positive consequences are made contingent on the child not having epileptic seizures—when healthy, epilepsy-free behaviors are nurtured—the frequency of seizures declines.

What has to be encouraged is not noisy behavior but just the opposite.

DIANE LEARNS INDEPENDENCE

Fortunately, many kinds of school difficulties escape this kind of labeling and are dealt with objectively with encouragement for the right kind of behavior. The case of the boy who didn't take pride in his schoolwork, forgot his coat and gloves on the playground, and couldn't manage to finish his papers on time is a "school" problem, but it was solved by his parents identifying as valuable behaviors his achievement in school and his giving appropriate attention to his belongings and homework.

Diane, for another example, was reported by her second-grade teacher to be unable to work independently.

"She works slowly at assigned tasks, although when I sit beside her and encourage her, she often does the task quickly and easily," the teacher said.

At times, Diane appeared to be unsure of herself, spoke in a shy, soft voice, and asked her teacher and friends to do things she should be able to do herself, like zipping up a zipper or putting her boots on.

"There's no question that Diane's a bright child," she continued. "She can do the work and she understands things well. The problem seems to lie in her unwillingness to do things on her own. She's not assertive, she'd rather rely on others. When she's supposed to be working on her own, she invariably looks to me or her classmates."

Luckily, the teacher took an objective look at her and didn't opt for an easy out by deciding that Diane needed psychological testing to uncover some sort of problem. Diane simply needed to be able to take the intelligence and capability she obviously had and turn them to good account by learning to be more independent and to have more confidence in the person she was.

In talking with her parents, it was clear that they catered to her excessively, and they admitted that since she was the youngest child, they and her older siblings encouraged her to be dependent at home. They helped her with her clothes and gave her plenty of opportunities to let them do things that she should do for herself.

When she went out into the wider world of school, however, behavior that was a matter of course at home took on a different meaning to teachers and fellow students; her lack of independence had a negative effect on her learning. In a class with many children making demands on the teacher's time, Diane's overdependence on others, if only to affirm her work as worthwhile, was unacceptable.

By putting the two viewpoints of Diane's behavior together, her teacher and her parents were able to see her difficulties clearly and to follow a system of praise and reward for grown-up, independent, responsible behaviors. At home that meant doing things without her parents' or brothers' and sister's help, and at school doing assigned work without the teacher at her side. At the same time, attention given to Diane immediately following "working-slowly" or "not-working" behaviors, or other less grown-up kinds of behavior, was kept to a minimum. Without that old payoff for being dependent, Diane's so-called learning problems became a thing of the past.

The point with school problems, from school phobia (not wanting to go to school at all) to behavior that disturbs an entire classroom, is to look at what is really going on. Again, understanding a child is less profitable in changing behavior than seeing the reality: what a child actually does and what kinds of rewards are given for the behavior to make it worthwhile.

The many teachers I work with have found that the system of praise and reward is highly effective, and it quickly becomes part of their whole philosophy of dealing with all the children in a class.

"When I get angry at the end of a rough day as I see Tom whispering across the aisle or Cathy bullying one of the other kids about something, I take a step back and remember that screaming isn't going to do anything but make Tom or Cathy the center of attention. I leave it at a reprimand, and try the next day to find something in Tom or Cathy to praise. It saves wear and tear on me, and it makes the children a little bit more proud of themselves and what they can do."

BABY LEARNS TO SLEEP

I once had a client whose ten-month-old baby got her up ten times a night. She had already been to a renowned child's sleep specialist and had tried a number of different approaches, all to no avail. "It's as though an alien has invaded his body," she said.

An infant obviously doesn't have much history, so it wasn't long before I learned there had been a series of family crises during the first two months of his life, and the mother had been with her son almost constantly during that early period. I later found another reason that she nurtured this unusual closeness-to-mother behavior: a long family history of fertility problems. When she gave birth she felt he was so special she wanted to hug him and nurture him and hold him all the time. "I keep telling myself I can't believe we made him."

The grandmother helped her, and because the boy was the first grandchild in many years, she did exactly the same thing, nurturing the same behavior. The mother couldn't even leave the child long enough to go to the bathroom; she literally had to take him with her when she used the toilet.

When I determined how dominant this pattern had become, I told the mother I wanted her to start nurturing distancing-from-mother behavior instead. I told her every time he was away from her, she should deliberately allow him to get used to separateness, no matter how noisy or painful it might prove to be; when they got back together she was to reward him with praise for being a big boy in her absence. "He's never going to stop loving you," I promised, "but unless you want him following you into the bathroom until you're an old woman, you need to reinforce his independence."

I described the analogy of when children learn to talk, a skill that improves in direct proportion to the extent talking is nurtured. I told her about the four-year-old boy whose parents came to me because he had a vocabulary of three words: yes, no, and that. He didn't need to learn anything else because those three words gave him everything he needed. When we nurtured imitative behavior to develop his language skills, within a month he had a vocabulary of over three hundred words and he hasn't stopped talking since.

The baby's mother followed the simple plan, and a few days later she returned to tell me, "It worked like a miracle. He sleeps from 8:00 P.M. until 8:00 A.M. without waking." She said it was as if her son had traded the demon for an angel.

A big part of what happened in this story, as in all the others, owes to the often astonishing power of the nurture response. The same principle applies to encouraging first words, first steps, and in this case the first evidence of healthy independence.

If people can have a hard time believing how well it works, it's usually because it's so easy.

Chapter Fifteen

DISCIPLINE AND THE "DIFFICULT CHILD"

When a mother and father are told by a professional that they have a "difficult child," the chances are that whatever they hear next won't be very helpful. Even if the therapist doesn't say outright that the child was born that way, that's the impression it makes on the parents, and the effect can be devastating. I can't count the number of parents over the years who have asked me, in one way or another, if their young child's problem behaviors were even treatable. "Maybe what we really need to hear is that not much can be done," they tell me, "—that we've got a problem and we're stuck with it. At least we know we tried, and that it's not our fault."

I've run into this attitude far more frequently since the publication of a book on so-called difficult children, which a number of parents have actually brought with them on their first visit. The bestseller describes a number of serious behavioral problems in young children, including severe, long-lasting temper tantrums, biting other children and even adults, throwing food at the table, frequently disrupting their parents' sleep by getting into their bed at night, crying too long and too often. The author suggests a number of responses, from laying down the law to various forms of pleading disguised as rational discourse, and not surprisingly they don't always get terrific results. The bottom line for readers of the book is that if the parents can't change their children, then what they *can* change is their own expectations as to how their children should act.

In all my years as a therapist, I've yet to meet a single child whose problem behaviors were solely the result of something they were "born with." And I've never had a case in which even the worst behavior didn't improve dramatically once the parents learned to alter their responses to disruptive behavior and to use the nurture response to encourage an appropriate repertoire of behaviors.

Any one of these examples of serious disruptive behaviors—including pushing, hitting, throwing food, and abusive or obscene language—has a number of such alternatives, and each cries out for immediate intervention.

One of the most important lessons in child-rearing is that no matter how parents respond to a child's behavior, they are nurturing *something*. If they inadvertently nurture violent outbursts, then the child will produce more violence. If they nurture pouting, then that's what they'll get back. Conversely, if the child is acting in any of these ways, it's because somewhere along the line there is a reward for that type of behavior. The same is obviously true of children who develop the best possible social and learning skills.

The question of discipline and punishment—for there are certainly occasions when they are necessary—is a difficult one. It doesn't follow that if praise builds positive behaviors, some form of punishment stops negative ones, especially if the punishment takes the form of "a good talking to"—the very kind of attention that centers on the child, giving him parental time and concern. A leading advice-giving columnist suggests sending a naughty child to his room for thirty minutes as punishment. It supposedly gives the child time to contemplate his misdeeds and, so the parents hope, to see the error of his ways. It is doubtful, however, that a half an hour, usually in a room filled with toys, will make the "punished" behavior occur less often. In fact, the only positive benefit would seem to be for the parents in that the child is out of sight for thirty minutes.

On the other hand, punishment in terms of a total absence of rewards can be highly effective if it is used sparingly. In addition, it should be used only for serious misdeeds, for example, cursing, hitting, and intentional destruction of property.

There are four criteria for punishment. Punishment should be:

1. Fair
2. Infrequent
3. Immediate
4. Brief

PUNISHMENT AND PARENTS

"I was punished as a child, and I didn't like it. I never want to punish anyone, especially my son."

The problem is, this mother has a child who very much needs to have limits clearly set. Roger does a lot of things that are serious, that have to be stopped when they occur. His mother admits that her method of dealing with serious behaviors is ineffectual.

Roger is consistently doing what he's told not to and typically refuses direct parental orders. He gets to his mother by saying, "You hate me. What kind of mother are you?" He hits his mother; he curses her. He hits other children.

"I can't bring myself to punish him, but I have to admit I'm building up a lot of resentment. I see mothers who say, 'Stop doing that,' and just with those words and the tone of their voice the children stop. The mothers don't even have to say, 'I don't like that, don't do it'—just one look, and the child doesn't do it anymore. If I say 'Don't do that' to Roger, he does it one more time. He's relentless."

Because of her inability to put a halt to the behaviors that trouble her, Roger and his mother face repeated battles that only create increasing feelings of resentment and anger between parent and child.

If Roger's mother wants to be able to stop him with a look or a few soft-spoken words, both of those actions have to be associated with a meaningful consequence. At the moment, Roger knows there's none.

The consequence can be many things: no attention at all, a reprimand, or a stronger form of punishment. If the look has to be followed by words, and then the words have to be followed by action, the sequence will be meaningful only if it takes place in rapid order.

"I DON'T WANT TO TALK ABOUT IT . . ."

Throughout this book, we have dealt with how to encourage positive behaviors with praise and reward, and how to examine behavioral problems to see the ways they have been given unintended encouragement.

When Cindy eggs on her parents with comments like "You don't love me; you hate me," they rush to reassure her that they certainly do love her. Their unfailing response is her reward; she has their attention—they give her their time and emotional energy.

Conversely, taking away these rewards makes the behavior less worthwhile. One perfectly good form of punishment is to withhold a reward, and for most behavioral problems a simple "I don't want to discuss it" is an effective nonreward that acknowledges the behavior and expresses disapproval.

That's different from completely ignoring a behavior, which is *not* effective. If parents say nothing at all, the child is likely to increase the shock value of the behavior until he or she *does* get a response. Behavior must be acknowledged, but it should not be followed by long reasoning sessions or reprimands.

"I DON'T WANT YOU TO DO THAT . . ."

Another step in nonreward that acknowledges a behavior and expresses disapproval is a brief, angry reprimand. Again, brevity is important; firmly resist being drawn into a discussion about the behavior.

Eddie is a problem at mealtimes, banging his fork on the table, kicking the table leg, dominating the meal with complaints and refusal to eat. Even as his parents have learned to give encouragement to the moments when he shows appropriate mealtime behaviors, he still continues those irritating behaviors. The response to them has to be not the long drawn-out arguments that have occurred in the past but a short angry comment: "I don't want you to do that" or "Eddie! Do not bang your fork."

This sort of reprimand, replacing a good deal of attention, effectively changes the feel of the environment, and while the appropriate behavior builds, the negative behavior tends to diminish, since rewards are minimized for negative behavior except for the few words that express strong disapproval.

TIME-OUT FOR SELF-CONTROL

Sometimes more forceful punishment is necessary, but keep in mind the guidelines of fair, infrequent, immediate, and brief.

If Eddie insists on upping the ante, there's no point in sending him to his room, typically a warehouse of toys, books, television, and other sources of pleasure, as it simply removes the child from a bad situation where he is unhappy and trades it for a good situation filled with rewards. The most effective technique is one that denies a child access to people, to the environment, to the many satisfactions in his world.

Time-Out from reinforcement is a near-total absence of rewards for three to five minutes. It is equivalent in part to the old-fashioned schoolroom method of sitting a child in a corner.

Here are four things Time-Out isn't:

- It isn't a form of play, in which the referee-parent is a part of the game.
- It isn't a form of distraction aimed at stopping offensive behavior by changing the subject.

- It isn't aimed at humbling, embarrassing, or causing pain.
- It isn't the parents acting out the same impulse of frustration and rage that they say is intolerable in the child.

Time-Out is a firm, decisive *consequence* of seriously offensive and out-of-control behavior. It interrupts a process that has gone wrong, and physically separates the child from his/her world. Don't expect the child to cool down; the purpose is to vividly demonstrate the laws of cause and effect. It's an extremely effective technique when used sparingly, but like any other strong medicine, its benefits decline with frequency and disappear completely with abuse.

When the parents of five-year-old Delia asked my advice in dealing with problems that frequently included her calling them obscene names and using physical violence, I developed guidelines for them.

First, when Delia engages in extremely disruptive behaviors such as kicking anyone, cursing Mother or Father, temper tantrums, or hitting either parent, they were to *immediately* tell her, "We do *not* _____ (kick, curse, scream, whatever)."

Next, they *quickly* take her by the hand, *saying nothing further,* and seat her in a small chair, facing a *blank* wall. This should be done only at home, and only in the presence of the immediate family (never is the purpose of any intervention to embarrass the child). If Delia screams or kicks while in the chair, or says she has to go to the bathroom, they should ignore her. If she attempts to leave the chair, a parent should be near enough to *quickly* (without saying a word) return her to the chair, avoiding a chase. If Delia pleads that she will be good, they should ignore her—not talk to her, not answer her questions or complaints no matter how creative, not even tell her to be quiet.

Delia must remain in the chair for a minimum of three minutes. If at the end of the three minutes she has been quiet during the last five seconds, quickly go to her, praise her, tell her she has been quiet and well behaved, and she may now leave the chair.

If at the end of four minutes Delia is kicking or screaming or even talking, you can reduce the seated-quietly behavior to just a couple of seconds. As soon as she has been quiet for this time, quickly go to her and tell her she has been quiet and well behaved, and she may now leave the chair.

The parents never allow Delia to leave the chair while misbehaving, and they never discuss the punishment afterward.

If afterwards Delia wants to discuss what has occurred, no dialogue is permitted. The only thing you may say is "We do not _____," followed by a restatement of the behavior being punished.

The judicious use of Time-Out is probably the best way a parent can discipline a child for serious infractions, because it demonstrates an obvious and immediate relationship between cause and effect. By contrast, the taking away of privileges for long periods of time (days, weeks, months) encourages deep feelings of resentment toward parents. Most of us know adults who still recall the most severe punishments of their childhood long after the offenses that produced them have been forgotten.

What do I mean when I say Time-Out is an effective punishment if used infrequently and for only the most serious behaviors? Any form of punishment used too often or for minimal cause stirs up anger and resentment toward parents and gradually destroys the bonds of affection between parents and child. Even when a relationship is 99 percent warmth and affection and 1 percent punishment, the ratio is too high on the punishment end of the scale. When Time-Out is used sparingly, as an immediate response to extreme behavior, it can eliminate that behavior.

MICHAEL'S TANTRUMS

Mr. and Mrs. Smith are parents of three-year-old Michael, a bright, energetic child who has been driving them crazy.

During the past year and a half, Michael has terrorized his family by having tantrums when things do not go his way. He is so impatient that when he wants his father's attention, he can't wait long enough even for him to put down whatever he happens to be holding. Michael writes on walls, hits, throws food at the table, has frequent tantrums, and his parents "can't take him anywhere."

The Smiths told me they had read "every difficult child book in the library" and contemplated having Michael tested for ADD; by the time they arrived in my office, they were frustrated and exhausted.

I met with them for six sessions, during which I gave them specific recommendations. Within two weeks after they started applying them to Michael, they were back—this time, relaxed, refreshed, and happy. They said their son was like a different child; the changes in the parents were at least as dramatic as the improvements they reported in their little boy.

Michael and his family overcame years of painful behavior in a very short time without expensive psychotherapy. What I taught the Smiths in just a few short weeks were the principles of positive parenting, and how to apply the appropriate consequences for serious negative behaviors.

Here is what I had told them.

RECOMMENDATIONS FOR MICHAEL

Step 1

List four to six specific examples weekly of behavior in which Michael acted like a big boy, doing appropriate things on his own and acting grown-up.

EXAMPLES:

   A. Dressing himself

   B. Handling disappointment calmly when things do not go his way

   C. Brushing his teeth before bed

   D. Helping his father bring in the firewood (a Mother Theresa behavior, thinking of the other person)

Step 2

Four to six times weekly, apply ABCD nurture response sequence.

Step 3

Time-Out:

1. Purchase a small, wooden/plastic chair.

2. Put this chair facing a blank wall in an easy-to-get-to room in the house—*not in Michael's bedroom.*

3. Do not explain to Michael why he is being put there. This method must be used *only in the home, only in the presence of the immediate family, and only for serious, destructive, dangerous behaviors such as*:

   A) Tantrums
   B) Hitting
   C) Biting
   D) Writing on walls
   E) Throwing food at table

When you observe one of these behaviors:

1. Immediately take Michael by the hand and say, *"We do not _____"* (hit, etc.). *You must use the words, "We do not . . ."*

2. Seat him quickly in the small chair facing the blank wall.

3. Stay one to three feet from him all the time he is in the chair.

4. If he attempts to leave the chair, *without saying a word* gently return him to the chair with your hands.

5. If he yells, screams, kicks the wall, curses, or says he has to go to the bathroom, *ignore him*. Don't say a single word.

6. Michael must remain in the chair for a minimum of three minutes.

   Do not set a kitchen timer. Do not use an egg timer. Do not tell him how long it will be—for all he knows, it will be three hundred minutes.
   Do not say "Be quiet, sit still." Say nothing.

7. If he tries to talk to you, *Do not answer him—not a word.*

8. After three minutes, wait until he has been seated quietly for five seconds. Then turn to him and tell him he has been quiet and well-behaved and that he may now leave the chair. (While still in the chair if he continues to act up for more than four minutes, then let him up after just one or two seconds of quietly seated behavior.) *Never allow him to leave the chair unless he has been seated quietly.*

9. If he refuses to leave the chair, say, "You may leave whenever you wish."

10. Above all, *avoid a chase*. A chase is fun; this is not fun time.

THE ABCD'S OF POSITIVE REINFORCEMENT

Obviously, bringing up a child involves far more than punishment, and I never give parents advice on discipline without first telling them about the ABCD's and other recommendations for nurturing positive behavior that would make punishments unnecessary. (Also see Chapter 5 under "Communicating Values.")

A typical case in which I used this approach involved five-year-old Christine, described by her parents as "angry, full of tantrums, very demanding, with a very intense personality."

Not surprisingly, most of the tantrums were the result of things not going quite the way Christine had in mind. When her mother gave her a muffin spread with peanut butter instead of dairy butter, Christine flipped out. She erupted during a bath because she didn't want to share the tub with her sister. She made a scene when her mother set a schedule for her getting dressed. These incidents were occurring at the rate of once or twice a day—somewhat improved, the parents said, from their peak during the Terrible Two's, but still discouraging. They told me a big part of the problem was Christine's rivalry with her younger sister.

The first thing we did was set the parents' goals in coming to me with their problem. They wanted Christine to be more responsive to the needs of others, which they defined as "to start listening." They wanted to get rid of the anger in the house, and in its place they wanted everyone to be happy. They wanted the girls to play well together and to get along.

The further we got into the specifics of the case, the more it became obvious that the two biggest factors in Christine's behavior were her competition with the younger sister, and frustration when things didn't go her way. Accordingly, I advised the parents to keep a journal of specific instances of sibling caring by Christine; caring for anyone besides herself—Mother Theresa behaviors; and taking small disappointment calmly. It didn't have to be a minute-by-minute diary of her every mood; I told them they should try to note four to six examples weekly.

In the course of the following weeks, the parents saw and noted a number of such positive moments: Christine helping feed her crying baby sister during a hectic mealtime, responding quickly when told it was time to go to bed, being attentive and loving to her grandmother during a visit. They then followed the ABCD sequence (Chapter 5) of positive nurture.

As Christine's positive actions accrued praise and encouragement, they began to become more commonplace, eventually displacing the other, negative ways in which she had related to her little sister and to everyone else around her.

Chapter Sixteen

INVESTING IN THE UNSEEN

Do you remember the adage about the fruit never falling far from the tree? There is a point in all of our lives when we begin to hear it in a different way, when we shift our focus from our parents to our children. For those who came before, we are the fruit; for those who follow, we have become the tree.

One nice thing about that saying is that is doesn't make any claims for whether genetics has a greater influence than environment. It simply says that there are family patterns, for good or bad, and they pass through generations.

The first fruit in recorded history, the one from the tree in the Garden of Eden, was labeled Knowledge. It gave Adam and Eve, alone among all creation, the ability to distinguish good from evil. Theologians point to that event as the moment in which the human animal received free choice, and with it the responsibility for our souls. Until then, Adam and Eve had no reason to procreate—in fact, apparently had paid no special attention to their anatomical differences—perhaps because being made in the image of their Creator, they assumed they were immortal. So the eating of the fruit of the Tree of Knowledge was also the beginning of the human race.

That's what this book is about, because that is what life is about. We are still responsible for our souls. And we stand in the line of generations.

THE SILENT POWER OF NURTURE

B. F. Skinner has observed that the effects of positive reinforcement are silent, and that even their most dramatic consequences do not make themselves known immediately. In common with all the other forms of delayed gratification, parents must have vision, confidence, and the willingness to persist in their efforts based, at least in the beginning, on a faith in things unseen. Sometimes the process can test our patience, but if the exercise is good for a child's character, no doubt it strengthens our own as well.

Otherwise, the implications of Skinner's observation are frightening. If the negative focus of our world, including our tendency toward violence, is the result of the fact that the process is silent, then most of human behavior, in common with the behavior of all of the other animals standing lower on the phylogenetic scale, is under the influence of immediate consequences. When people favor behaviors leading to instant positive results, such as eating the marshmallow now, acts and decisions that produce delayed gratification will occur less often.

As for human caring, warmth, concern for others, even planning for our own future or the spiritual well-being of our children, all these behaviors will receive less nurture because they have silent consequences in that their results are beyond our view and in some instances beyond our lifetimes. If people can't delay gratification when the reward is out of sight, even if the benefit is guaranteed, then Eden might as well have never happened.

For readers of this book, the good news is that the delay is seldom very long. When I work with parents who are having problems with their children, it is not uncommon for radical improvement to occur in a child's behavior within weeks—or in some cases even within days. These changes don't happen by chance; they're the specific, predicted results of written recommendations that I give to the parents, teaching them how to praise, love, and nurture their children for positive behaviors.

Raising happy children means creating the conditions for happy adults, who find the satisfactions of life within their grasp instead of always eluding them.

One mother said to me recently when discussing her son's behavioral problems, "What do I want for him? I just want him to be happy." It's what we all want for our children, and the way to have happy children is to give them the behaviors that mean happiness and create feelings of self-worth that last a lifetime: being a good friend, knowing the satisfactions of responsibility, having an eagerness to seek out knowledge, and possessing a sense of caring.

In the course of my practice, when radical change occurs, sometimes parents who helped make it happen by giving their children a thoughtful, highly focused program of systematic nurture will attribute the results to nothing more deliberate than a new haircut, a school vacation or the onset of spring. If that happens, I tell them the Thorazine story.

It took place during a meeting of a review panel that I attended at the Veteran's Hospital in Brockton, Massachusetts; a man who had been a patient in psychiatric hospitals for seventeen years was being considered for discharge. All of the people who had been in contact with him were sitting around a large table, and they took turns questioning him to see if he was ready to face the world on his own. He answered every one of their questions as normally as you or I might have answered them.

The final question was from the psychiatrist in charge. "You've been in psychiatric hospitals for over seventeen years, and now you're up for discharge," he started. "That's a pretty big change. How do you think it happened? What's the main reason?"

The man nodded responsively and his answer sounded as normal as everything else he had told the panel. He replied that it was because of the strength he had been given by the Lord—God had healed him, and that new strength was now about to set him free. "After all I've been through, after all my family has endured, the Lord has answered all our prayers."

The doctor brought his hand down on the table. "This man will not be discharged," he said, ending the interview.

Two weeks later, we were all back in the meeting room: same discharge conference, same patient, same psychiatrist. The patient was as logical and coherent as he had been two weeks before. The difference was in his response to the last question, "Why do you think you're about to be discharged?"

He answered in four words. "Because of the Thorazine."

This time, the discharge was granted.

What the psychiatrist was attempting to communicate to the patient was that it was not God who was responsible for his recovering from psychosis or for his new-found ability to function outside the hospital. It was his medication, the very powerful tranquilizer Thorazine. Since he had to take Thorazine every day to maintain a life outside the hospital, he needed all the encouragement the psychiatrist could give him in continuing to take the medication. It was the Thorazine, not God, who would keep him out and keep him healthy—and if he stopped taking the drug because he'd decided to depend on God instead, he'd soon be back in the hospital.

It's the same way with nurture. If parents systematically nurture positive behaviors in a child, they often find it difficult to believe the dramatic changes that occur in so short a period of time. They act as though the improvement occurred for some other reason. Unlike Thorazine, the benefits of appropriate nurture will last a lifetime, and the need to continue that nurture gradually decreases with time.

The foundation for the many years between adolescence and old age is laid in the first dozen years of life, when the group of behaviors that we might call the personality of the individual is learned with the guidance of parents.

If being home on time is considered grown-up in a ten-year-old, it will be thought so by the sixteen-year-old. If answering the telephone and taking a good message is a way of being responsible in someone who's six or seven, the seventeen-year-old is going to know without thinking that he is responsible for fulfilling those obligations. If a small child respects the feelings and property of others because it's a caring behavior that is grown-up, the teenage boy or girl is going to behave in the same way. Thoughtfulness in children means thoughtful adults, happy marriages where husband and wife don't need a program of caring days to show how they feel. Thoughtful adults mean parents who will in turn teach thoughtfulness to their children. Children who have been nurtured in thirst-for-learning behaviors will become adults who don't stop learning, even though they are finished with their formal schooling.

In time, the parents are unable to escape the evidence that *a process is going on.* They recognize these changes as the rewards of their actions for the long-term benefit to their children and the family as a whole, actions that at the outset were guided by a faith in things unseen.

For good or bad, children continue to claim their birthrights and the legacies of their generation.

Silently, the fruit keeps falling near the tree.